I think you'll love Something More. *Pastor Jason Stonehouse has written a very practical, personal book, using the truths of another practical, personal Book—the Bible. So if you're a little "stalled out" with God these days, or just need some down-to-earth ideas and encouragement,* Something More *will deliver. Plus, there's an additional bonus: you'll make a new friend in Jason himself, as he transparently shares his own successes and failures (some quite humorously)—things that will make you laugh, ponder, pray, and really get moving in your faith journey.*

RICK MATTSON, INTERVARSITY STAFF AND AUTHOR OF *FAITH IS LIKE SKYDIVING: AND OTHER MEMORABLE IMAGES FOR DIALOGUE WITH SEEKERS AND SKEPTICS*

Jason Stonehouse is a gifted pastor, teacher, and counselor who relates to his readers as a genuine, caring friend. Jason has "been there, done that" in his own spiritual journey and in Something More, *he shares the keys to true Christian growth that he's learned along the way. If you've felt as if something is missing in your spiritual life and are longing for something more, this book is for you!*

DR. BILL MAIER
CLINICAL PSYCHOLOGIST AND RADIO HOST

Jason's story is one of so many pastors. You will love getting to hear his heart for God as well as how he is stewarding that to lead His local church to prevail not just maintain. I love it when pastors share vulnerabilities and the lessons learned from life-shaping turning points.

DOUG PARKS, CO-FOUNDER AND CEO INTENTIONAL CHURCHES

If your Christian faith experience is dry or rote or superficial, Something More *is the book for you! Jesus' sacrifice was not just for heaven someday. In* Something More, *pastor Jason Stonehouse provides a roadmap to adventure, purpose, and fulfillment in our lives now, by understanding and fully embracing the "something more" that Jesus died to give us.*

JIM GUSTAFSON, FORMER GRACE CHURCH ELDER AND BIBLE TEACHER

SOME
THING
MORE

PURSUING THE LIFE
YOU WERE MADE TO LIVE

JASON STONEHOUSE

bookVillages

DEDICATION

For the people of Grace Church in Roseville, MN

ACKNOWLEDGMENTS

I am in awe of the grace, mercy and love that has been lavished on me by Jesus.

I am thankful to my best friend and wife, Lisa, whose continual love, encouragement, and partnership fuels me forward and is the one person I always want to spend time with doing absolutely nothing or anything. I really don't want to leave out my incredible daughters—Jessica, Sydney, and Christina who've been in this whole process with me and who I am so grateful I get to do life with.

Kim Kankiewicz did an incredible job as editor and really made these sentences make sense—thank you! Rick Mattson & Jim Gustafson served as readers and collaborators on several sections—thank you! I appreciate your friendship and partnership in ministry.

I am grateful, too, for my staff team at Grace who truly make coming to work one of my favorite things to do. You are all all-stars in my book! I feel so much support as a pastor from our elders and really from the whole congregation at Grace—you guys are awesome!

This book has been in development for close to twenty years, and so I am grateful to all the people who God used to shape me into who I am today. I think of pastors, friends, students, mentors, my sister, Sherri, extended family and people who believed in me when others didn't. My grandfather, Sidney

Langford, was an inspiration and example for me and propelled me forward. And my parents, Phil and Ginny Stonehouse, have modeled for me this life of authenticity and belief and I can't thank God enough for the chance to have them as my parents and friends!

Thank YOU for reading this book. I pray that you enjoy it as much as I enjoyed writing it.

CONTENTS

FOREWORD

Jason takes you on his journey in this book, but then does something deeper. He takes you on your own journey, a journey we all need to make.

When I was in my twenties, I worked in law in downtown Toronto. I was surrounded by successful people. Lots of lawyers working in office towers, driving expensive cars, living the life most people only dreamed of. Ditto with bank executives, stock brokers and many others.

What also struck me was that despite all the success people had, they almost all wanted something more. And the more successful they got in their career, the more they realized their work or success couldn't deliver what they longed for. They had everything, but they felt like they had nothing.

I've never forgotten that, and to some extent, that *is* the struggle.

Even in ministry and life, how much is enough? Your church can never be big enough, your faith never deep enough, your marriage never rich enough. There's gotta be something more.

Jason takes you on a journey through this book that I hope will show you where more lives, and exactly how Jesus came to bring us so much more. It's a journey every one of us needs to take. I'm so grateful Jason helps us explore how to do that.

CAREY NIEUWHOF
AUTHOR, *LASTING IMPACT*
FOUNDING PASTOR, CONNEXUS CHURCH

INTRODUCTION
There's Gotta Be Something More

On a Sunday in March 1989, I had my first wake-up call. I was sixteen years old, and we had reached the age when we high school students broke free of our parents and sat with our friends during church services. Naturally, we chose to sit in the very last row of the balcony. The only way we could have been further from the music and message is if we'd been sitting in our cars (or more accurately our parents' cars) listening to the service on the radio. At least we were all taking notes while the pastor preached. Well okay,

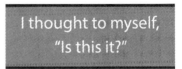

I thought to myself, "Is this it?"

we were all writing, but our notes had nothing to do with the sermon. They were handwritten conversations like *What are you doing after church today?* and the thoughtful response *My parents are making me go to lunch with them! Ugh!* For 35 minutes, the notes went back and forth. "Can you give this to Rob?" "Tell Becky I want an answer on this one."

For some reason I couldn't identify, I wasn't into the note passing that Sunday. I felt like I was having a kind of out of body experience. As I looked over this row of 25 high school students—some giggling, some pretending to listen, and others just zoned out—I thought to myself, "Is this it?"

Here we were, young people filled with potential and

gifted with passions. Most of us could quote Scripture, tell the stories of our faith, and even get excited about the next youth group event. And yet church and by extension our faith had become a place we gathered, a social group we identified with, an opportunity to find an acceptable date, but little more. Something important was missing. If the others didn't feel it, I sure did that day.

It wasn't a Christian heritage that I was missing. Growing up in a New Jersey suburb 20 minutes from New York City, I was raised in the church by a family of believers in Jesus. My grandparents had been missionaries in Africa for 20 years before returning to the States to lead a missions organization for another two decades. My parents talked freely about God, immersed us in church activities, led devotions after dinner, and served as examples of church-going, upright, moral living. I attended the Christian version of Boy Scouts from a young age and transitioned right into youth group. I quickly became a student leader, taught Bible studies, and even started one at my public high school. I tell you this to let you know that if there were Christian experiences to be had, I had them. I was blessed with dedicated Sunday school teachers, outstanding role models of faith, and opportunities to grow through rallies, events, youth speakers, and mission trips. I did regular devotions for five to six years of junior high and high school and was growing spiritually. And I wasn't alone. Most members of my high school youth group had similar experiences. Yet something was missing.

And if that was the case for us, people with all the benefits of church and a religious heritage, then what about people who came to faith later in life or even those who see no value in the things of faith? You see, while I was feeling the need for more as a Christian, the search for something more is universal. Within every human being is a hunger, a desire. We try to fill it with all kinds of things, but nothing seems to satisfy our need. We don't have to look far to find stories of broken relationships, substance abuse, risky behavior, thrill seeking, corporate ladder rising, job jumping, and other evidence of a world that longs for something more yet continually comes up short in the search. The ironic thing is that when people who are far from God express their longing for something more, we tell them to go to church. Some do, only to find that even some of our most vibrant churches are filled with people secretly wondering, "Is this really all that life and faith offer? Am I missing something more?"

Sitting in my pew in the last row of the balcony, feeling that ache for more, was one of a few experiences in a four-month time frame that changed the direction of my life. In the same time period, I attended youth retreats with passionate speakers who sparked deep thinking. And then there were the weekly trips to a park near my house for "walks with God." On these walks, while I didn't hear an audible voice, I *felt* God speak. In 90 minutes, God connected a bunch of pieces in my mind and showed me a clear next step.

Until that point, I was set to attend college to major in business administration. I planned to become a business owner or hotel manager and of course do a little ministry on the side. I mean I was a Christian! But I couldn't shake that balcony moment. From the start, I knew the experience wasn't just about me. It wasn't just my own quest. I wanted to help others. Maybe if I'm honest, I felt a little self-righteous. I thought maybe *those* people could use some change. I saw these poor high school students and their need for someone to show them a better way! So I shifted my direction toward Bible college and youth ministry because someone had to help these poor kids, and kids like them, to see what faith and life could be. (I am being slightly facetious here.)

I studied hard and became immersed in the culture of Bible college and the Christian "bubble." I loved my experience in Bible college and I learned a ton, yet I'm not sure how much I really paid attention to my own heart in the midst of it. I prepared messages—we called them "youth talks"—that spoke of getting "on fire" for God, not settling, and embracing a bigger life in Jesus. I meant every word, at least to the best of my understanding back then. But little did I know I was only at the beginning of what would be a lifelong journey, a journey that continues as I write to you today.

My first full-time youth ministry position was at a church in New Jersey. I went in with lots of vision and big dreams of success. What I didn't know about being a pastor (or even a Christian for that matter) I made up for with energy, passion, and a drive for something great. I was calling students to embrace a bigger life and not settle for living on the surface, pretending to be something they weren't. I wanted so desperately for others to have a life of something more. But what I yearned for others to have, I had little time or energy to cultivate for myself. I began to ignore, rationalize, or conceal my faults, insecurities, weaknesses, and sin. I was a pastor, and we all know that pastors don't struggle. If they do have faults, they certainly don't talk about them. I know that's not true, but it's what I believed back then. It drove me to hide, to take cover behind a perfect image of what I thought everyone wanted, even *needed* me to be.

The perfect mirage of a life I was living came to a screeching halt in my fourth year of full time ministry. One of the married female volunteers in our youth ministry confessed romantic feelings toward me, a single youth pastor. This threw me off guard. I didn't know what to do. What she said cracked my self-image and the image I was trying to present. Instead of seeking counsel (which would have added witnesses), I told no one and did nothing, except to double down on managing my public, "pastoral" image. Looking back, it seems this was one of God's first efforts to convince me that what I was pursuing was an empty shell, certainly not the something more He had for me.

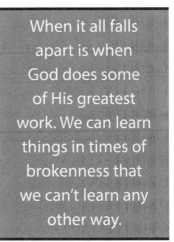

When it all falls apart is when God does some of His greatest work. We can learn things in times of brokenness that we can't learn any other way.

But I did not get God's message. I sincerely tried to live the best way I could, but I always projected an image that was better than reality. One of my supervisors, who I'm pretty sure didn't want me around anymore, heard that I'd covered up the fact that this woman had confessed feelings towards me. Even though I had not acted on or reciprocated her feelings, this supervisor was convinced it was time for me to go. He began a witch hunt, asking everyone who knew me of anything I'd said or done that was hurtful or offensive or less than honest. A case was built that resulted in my resignation.

As I look back now, I know that with some wise mentoring and counsel, and some healthy humility on my part, this episode could have been avoided or even turned into a positive growth experience. But I was still managing the external image. God did end up using this situation in a good way, but not before I endured the most painful period in my life. In what felt like an instant, my life, my career, and my faith were crashing around me. My resignation left over 150 students wondering what had happened and questioning their own faith. My lifelong dream, that I had trained and prepared for, was over. Meanwhile, I was left without a job, without a career, and without an identity. I wondered what I really believed. Was this what it meant to be a part of a church? Was this is how we treated people who struggle? Forget something more. At this point, I would have settled for "something."

You see, I had come to regard my accomplishments in ministry as my worth, my value, the very essence of who I was. But when these performance-driven externals were taken away, everything I thought I was and stood for collapsed. When it all falls apart is when God does some of His greatest work. We can learn things in times of brokenness that we can't learn any other way. And thankfully God provided a great counselor and some good friends and family to walk through this time with me.

While my faith was slowly being restored, this low point left me wondering about the future. This crisis of faith and identity awoke in me another moment of decision, another realization that "there's gotta be more than this!" This time it was not a passion for someone else's growth or experience. This time it was personal. Who was I going to be? If I never had the chance to serve in full-time ministry again, what was my faith going to be? Who was Jesus to me, really?

I made a decision: If God ever gave me the chance to serve again, things would be different. I would be different. I wouldn't pretend to be something I was not, or to have something that I didn't have. And if I never returned to full-time ministry, my faith would be just as vital and life-giving as if I had.

At such points in our lives, things get real. It's no longer about what someone else wants or says. It's you and God and reality. I began discovering that a real faith is possible, regardless of your environment, your family, or your church. There is a way to walk with God through the good and the bad. There is a way to find hope when things look hopeless. There is a way to find direction when you're confused. There is a way to claim an authentic identity that isn't swayed by others' opinions or perceptions. There is life: true, abundant, and full life for everyone. I want to share with you some of the answers I found and walk with you on this critically important journey. Whether you have a strong pedigree of faith or you've just come to faith recently—there is more! Whether you've worn faith as a uniform to get you into the club or sworn off faith as irrelevant and not for you—there is more! Whether you've seen God as a cosmic killjoy or a vending machine of blessings, an emergency life preserver or a ticket into heaven—there is more!

Unfortunately, many of us have settled. We've settled into a watered-down version of Christianity that reduces faith to something we do, a place we go, or a set of self-help principles to live by. Some of us may see our faith as a hobby. Others of us have dismissed or resigned ourselves to a God who has little interest in our lives and is judgmental, restrictive, and out of date. Still others of us have linked God and Christianity to a person or group of people who have let us down, and have therefore written off any value in pursuing more of this God.

I set out to write this book more than 15 years ago, hoping to inspire students to embrace the faith I longed for as a student. A lot has happened since then. I married my best friend, Lisa. I became the dad of three amazing daughters, Jessica, Sydney, and Christina. I was given the privilege of providing direction for Grace Church in Roseville, Minnesota, as the lead pastor. And do you know what I'm discovering? The yearning for something more is not just a student issue. I see single adults, married folks, moms, dads, and even grandparents who long for something more. And that's what I hope you will discover with me in this book.

> There is a life with God that He intends for all, but few ever realize.

Personally, while I've learned a ton, I still know deep down that God has more for me and my life than what I'm experiencing today. I want to be in the best place for Him to do His greatest work, and I want you to be there too. This is not just a "nice to have" kind of thing. I believe it's the life we were originally designed to experience but aren't!

As a pastor for more than 20 years and a Christian for more than 30, I see far too many people who, for whatever reason, have settled into a version of faith that is downright wrong, a little removed or far shy of God's intention. While you may not relate to all the details of my story, I do believe you need this journey. There is a life with God that He intends for all, but few ever realize. So don't miss this! There's a hope that goes beyond coffee-cup Bible verses and empty platitudes. There's a love that reaches deeper than a sappy worship song and is strong enough for the lowest of our lows. There's a faith that sees the unseen, believes the unbelievable, and reaches the unreachable. And while I'm not there yet, I'm not stopping until I get there. Join me on this search for something more!

Chapter 1

A "SOMETHING MORE" PERSPECTIVE:
Embrace Life with God as a Process

Before we get started, make sure you've read the introduction. I know, I know, you want to get to the good stuff. To be honest, I typically skip a book's introduction too. I mean you picked up this book because you saw something on the back cover that sparked your interest or someone told you it would be worth reading. You don't need to be sold on the book. But this introduction isn't a sales pitch; it's a foundation. It's my true story, a story that has shaped both my life and this book! So if you haven't yet, go read it. We'll wait for you.

Okay, let's go.

"As is." That's how cars, furniture, and even houses are sold. Typically it's because the seller either does not want to make repairs or feels that you, the buyer are getting such a bargain that you should do your own fixing. It's something we all know, and think we understand; and without examining it, we think God works that way too. But no: God loves me "as is." He died for me "as is." But He is not satisfied with me "as is." All God's people are fixer-uppers, and He is the Master Craftsman. He intends some upgrades for us or, better said, some restorative work. He looks at our lives impacted by sin and knows we could be something more! Unfortunately many of us live our lives with an "as is" mentality. We tell people, "What you see is what you

> If we're satisfied with life and faith "as is," we will never experience something more.

get." Or if we're a little older we say, "I've been this way for so many years, I'm not about to change now." And sure, we've all encountered people along our journey who always seem to want to change us. A little pushback is healthy in those situations. But our resistance to change may have more to do with the fact that change is scary and, let's be honest, can be downright hard. This is all complicated by some theological misunderstandings that we'll get to in a minute. The bottom line is if we're satisfied with life and faith "as is," we will never experience something more.

COME AS YOU ARE

First, the theological issue at stake. God loves us, just as we are. You may have heard a preacher say, "There's nothing you can do to get God to love you any more than He loves you right now, and there's nothing you can do to get God to love you any less than He loves you right now." Recently I've restated that to say that God loved us and accepted us before we ever did one good thing for Him (or bad thing against Him, for that matter). That is a true statement, and maybe the most freeing one you've heard all day. Expressed so powerfully in Romans 5:8, the great message of the Gospel is that "while we were still sinners, Christ died for us!"

There is no mud room in God's house. In Minnesota, where my family and I live, most homes have a mud room, a space a little bigger than a closet where you can take off your snow clothes in the winter or your muddy shoes in the spring. The mud room is a place to clean yourself up and leave the mud behind before entering the rest of the house. Some people think that God has a mud room—that as humans who are not all we should be, we need to clean up our act first to be acceptable to God. People start attending churches thinking they'll earn points with God, offsetting their past failures. But again, the message of the Gospel is that Jesus died *while* we were sinners. In fact, if we don't meet Jesus *in* our sin, we really miss His amazing gift. It's the humility to recognize our great need for Jesus' sacrifice and receive it by faith as a gift, something we could never earn or attain by ourselves, that connects us to God. So "as is" is the only way we can come to Jesus. Through Jesus, God redeems us "as is."

One way to discern whether you've come to Jesus "as is," receiving salvation as a gift, is to ask yourself, "If I were to die and stand at the gates of heaven and God asked, *Why should I let you in?* what would I say?" I asked this question during premarital counseling with a couple in my church. The groom, Adam (not his real name), was one of the nicest guys you would ever meet. He answered, "I always try to do the right thing, I try to be kind to everyone, and I think I'm a pretty loyal guy." Adam had attended church since he was a kid, had never really had a rebellious phase, and here he was sitting in a pastor's office next to the girl he loved and wanted to marry. But as I listened to his answer, I heard a lot of religion, but not a lot of what God is looking for in the hearts of those who are truly His.

Some of the scariest words of Jesus are found in Matthew 7:21-23: "Not everyone who says to me, 'Lord, Lord,' will enter the kingdom of heaven, but the one who does the will of my Father who is in heaven. On that day, many will say to me, 'Lord,

Lord did we not prophesy in your name, and cast out demons in your name, and do many mighty works in your name?' And then will I declare to them, 'I never knew you; depart from me, you workers of lawlessness.'"

As a pastor, while I want everyone to be assured of their salvation and faith, I am also continually wary of giving a false hope by calling people to a public decision of faith only to see them fade away after some time. Salvation occurs only when we transfer trust. We no longer trust in ourselves, our works, or our pedigree, but we fully trust in what Jesus did for us, dying as our substitute and sacrifice on the cross. Yes Jesus is love. Yes Jesus modeled a life worth emulating. Yes Jesus accepted everyone, taught amazing sermons, and asked people to follow Him. But most importantly, Jesus came to die for us. Our sin separates us from God. There is only one way to be reconnected to Him, and that's to trust—not just in who Jesus is, not just in His great example, but in what He did for us. His bloody death was necessary because sin always requires death. It's our complete and utter dependence on what He did for us that connects us to Him. The life we then live is our response to His gift.

I was so excited to see this message not only click for Adam, but prompt a decision on his part. Adam realized that the faith he was living was based on his church attendance and moral life. He realized this had to be personal, that He had to personally connect with Jesus, and He did. Later at the wedding, as I pronounced Adam and his bride husband and wife, I knew that they were beginning their marriage with

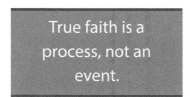

True faith is a process, not an event.

Jesus at the center of their lives and their relationship. They've been an active part of our church for years since then and are experiencing something more as a result of their faith.

The reason I spend so much time on this is that before you can move toward something more, you need to make sure that what you have is really "something," not an empty formula, fire insurance, or a religious club membership. True faith in the Gospel of Jesus Christ is a personal, humble response of trust in what Jesus did for us. True faith is a beginning, not an end. True faith is a process, not an event.

LIFE IN PROCESS

The knowledge that no one's perfect, and that Jesus loves us regardless of what we do, can quickly become an excuse for never growing. We have a saying at our church that didn't originate with us, but we like it: "Come as you are, but don't stay that way." In one phrase we try to capture the truth of the Gospel: we must approach God without pretense, raw, humble, and honest (and often broken, burned out, and lots of other adjectives). Once we receive the gift of God, the sacrifice of Jesus in our place, we are invited into a plan of transformation where we will grow to be more like Jesus and experience the fullness He intends.

Unfortunately, many people become "Christians" out of a fear of hell or wanting to settle their eternity issue, or they're moved by an emotional worship service and therefore look at their faith as an event but not a process. This, I believe, has created a faith community filled with people who think they are saved but may not be! I've met many regular church attenders, many shining examples of moral behavior, who seemed to place their eternal security more on their own behavior and attendance record than on Jesus.

Humility is the key characteristic that begins our relationship with Jesus and sustains that relationship over time. I love how Paul puts it in Galatians 3:3: "Are you so foolish? Having begun by the Spirit, are you now being perfected by the flesh?" He's asking why we think that, having become Christians by admitting our need and depending on the Spirit's work in our lives, we can take it from there. As if you and I could rid our lives of sin and become like Jesus, essentially without Jesus! We are dependent on a Savior to bring us into relationship with God and a Sanctifier to bring about godly change. But if we adopt an attitude of humility, teachability, and willingness to surrender to God's work in us, we will be well served for this journey!

To begin our journey toward something more, we must embrace the attitude that life in Christ is a process. And while Jesus is the "founder and perfecter of our faith" (Hebrews 12:2) and the one who will bring to completion the good work He began in us (Philippians 1:6), you and I have the responsibility and privilege of cooperating and moving forward with the work of God's Spirit in us. A life in process is perpetually in motion.

Having grown up in the church, I've seen too many who resist this idea of being a person in process. I don't know whether it's because the church environment discourages us from talking about our shortcomings or simply because we want to believe that we're better than we actually are. In the first several years that I served at Grace Church, our commitment to fostering a "life in process" environment brought significant change and transition. This transition caused many to look elsewhere for church because what we were becoming was not what they signed up for. Others left because of music styles, programming shifts, and relational loss. It was hard to lose so many great people. In spite of it all, one of the changes I've observed is that we've become a place where it's normal to have not arrived, to struggle with living the life we are called to live. We frequently say that there are no perfect people allowed at our church; if you are perfect, we want you to leave because you'll make the rest of us feel uncomfortable! Our care pastor, Steve Crane, who has been at Grace Church for years, said, "We've always had people who struggled. Now we've just made it okay to say so."

When we don't embrace a life in process, we end up lying or faking it. No one is perfect, and yet in too many churches we seem to propagate the idea that we've all arrived. We walk around with plastic smiles afraid to share the reality that our marriage is in crisis, or our private life is plagued by lust, or our anger is destroying relationships. This plastic existence makes us feel more alone, powerless, and empty than if we'd just stayed home.

> The New Testament regards spiritual growth as normal, not the exception to the rule.

Another effect of resisting a life in process is that we become stuck or stagnant. Imagine a child who arrives at the end of her third grade year and proclaims to her mom, "I'm not going to fourth grade. I like third grade. My teacher is great, I like what we're learning, and I'd like to learn it again!" As the rest of her class grows and eventually graduates high school, she sits in a third grade classroom long after she's outgrown her seat and her teacher has retired. That's a ridiculous scenario, but unfortunately it's not far from the truth for some folks in our churches. We keep showing up for "class" to learn the same things, never putting them into practice and never stepping out in faith. We may end up getting smarter, but not necessarily better. We plateau in our faith and begin critiquing the church, like perpetual third graders complaining about boredom while criticizing any change.

By contrast, those who embrace life as a process are continually looking to learn, grow, and live the life that God has called them to live. A third grade faith isn't going to cut it in an adult world. As we take steps forward, our faith grows. We learn to trust God more, pray like it matters, and sacrifice ourselves for the sake of Christ. We'll talk more about that a little later.

The attitude that spiritual life is a process is the foundation for discovering something more. Here are three aspects of a life in process that will shape our thinking moving forward.

1. In a life in process, MOVEMENT IS NORMATIVE.

In 1 Corinthians 3, Paul is surprised that the Corinthian believers are not ready for "solid food" and that he can only give them milk. This implies that movement and spiritual growth should have been happening all along but weren't. Hebrews 5:12 states, "...by this time you ought to be teachers, [but instead] you need someone to teach you again." The point is that movement and growth are expected, and it's odd when they aren't. Often in churches, we assume that those who are growing spiritually are either new believers or superstar Christians. Yet the New Testament regards spiritual growth as normal, not the exception to the rule. If we're ever going to discover something more, movement must become our norm. You may have heard the expression, "It's easier to steer a moving car than a parked one." Church should be a learning environment to be steered, not jump-started!

I love the story (who knows if it's true, but it's still a good one) of the pastor who preached a sermon one week that everyone loved. He then returned the next week and preached the exact same sermon. People wondered if he'd had a bad week and didn't have time to prepare something new, so they gave him the benefit of the doubt and listened politely. But then week three came and once again he preached the same sermon. People in the church began to grumble, "What do we pay this guy for? Doesn't he have more than one sermon?" This went on for four or five weeks until the congregation had had enough. Finally someone in the church asked the pastor why he kept repeating the same sermon. He replied, "When you all start applying this sermon, we'll go on to the next one." Oh, if only I had the guts to do that!

Unfortunately it's become normal in church to desire new and deeper content every week, but with little attempt to actually apply what is taught. A "something more" kind of faith develops not just through more content, but through acting on what God reveals. We must embrace a mindset where spiritual movement is normative.

2. In a life in process, REFLECTION IS REGULAR.

We live in a world full of anxiety and stress, with people pushing and pulling and demanding more from us. We're always multitasking because we have so much to accomplish that we can't just do one thing. We can't just drive a car somewhere; we have to be texting, checking Facebook, eating an egg McMuffin, and shaving—all in a five-minute commute! Time for reflection has disappeared from our lives. I mean we can't even look out the window for a few minutes without feeling guilty because of all we need to do. The result of this pace of life is that we tend to be reactive, looking just to survive and telling ourselves, "Someday this will be different."

Probably one of the best takeaways from this chapter would be to incorporate regular times to reflect. I try to do this for a few hours every few weeks by going to a park or coffee shop to think and reflect, but it doesn't even have to be that long. You can turn off the radio in your car and spend ten minutes reflecting as you drive. Some people like to get up early and journal. Others find time to reflect while they exercise. These blocks of time need to be prioritized, however. In addition, I would strongly urge you to take more extended time for reflection at least once a month because it is that important to our growth. Who knows? It may be the one thing that turns it all around and sets you on a pathway to something more.

So what do you do to truly reflect? First off, you need to eliminate distractions. No internet, email, or electronics. Secondly, once you've created a quiet space, reflection is simply thinking deeply. It's giving serious thought to the deeper passions and purposes in your soul. It's paying attention to two realities: 1. Who God is and the work He's doing in the world (God's Story) and 2. Who you are and what you're doing, feeling, and thinking (Our Story). It's taking time to meditate on Scripture—reading, rereading, and thinking about God's intention, heart, and desired application. When it comes to "Our Story," I like to think back to my emotions. I ask myself things like, "Why did I feel that way when she said that?" or "What was driving me in that discussion?" or "Why is that so important to me?" We look at who God made us to be and evaluate how we're doing and what might be hindering our growth. We spend time understanding ourselves and our desires, and we pray, opening up our lives to allow God to speak into us.

One of my favorite chapters in the Gospels is Mark 1 because it shows us an incredibly busy season (or it may have been one busy day) in the life of Jesus. He's calling disciples, casting out demons, and healing people. Then in verse 35 and following we're told, "And rising very early in the morning, while it was still dark, he departed and went out to a desolate place, and there he prayed. And Simon and those who were with him searched for him, and they found him and said to him, 'Everyone is looking for you.'" It's as if Simon is saying, "Jesus, there's a lot going on and lots of people need your time and attention!" And then Jesus replies, "Let us go on to the next towns, that I may preach there also, for that is why I came out." While we don't know the content of His prayer, His example establishes a model for us: take time to reflect and pray, and you will be prepared for your next step.

Our next step might be an area of growth, an act of faith, a conversation, a sin to confess, a promise to embrace, or an encouragement to own. The reality is if we don't regularly reflect like this we will miss what God is doing, how God is leading, and what is happening in our own hearts! John Ortberg says it this way in his book *The Life You've Always Wanted*: "For many of us the great danger is not that we will renounce our faith. It is that we will become so distracted and rushed and preoccupied that we will settle for a mediocre version of it. We will just skim our lives instead of actually living them."

3. In a life in process, CHANGE IS CONSTANT.

Back in high school, I loved getting our yearbooks because it meant several days of loose class structures while we had our books signed by all our friends. Do you remember one of the most humorous, yet intended to be sincere comments written in a yearbook? "Don't ever change!" Seriously? My guess is that some of you have had reunions and get-togethers with high school friends who clearly took that advice. They're still reliving the same memories and acting like they did back then. They did what their yearbooks entries said—they never changed! The fact is if we don't change, we never become better. Obviously, not all change is good and I'm not advocating change just for variety. But intentional change, typically in response to a godly reflection time, can yield great results.

Consider Paul's words in Galatians 4:19: "My little children for whom I am again in the anguish of childbirth until Christ is formed in you." Or in Colossians 1:28: "Him [Christ] we proclaim, warning everyone and teaching everyone with all wisdom, that we may present everyone mature in Christ." These and countless other verses speak to the expectation of growth, change, and spiritual transformation in our lives. This means we should be able to look back to one year ago and name something that has changed in

> I must view my life as a continual restoration project where He is making me over to what I was originally designed to be.

us because of God's work. If I'm not learning to love God and love others more, year after year, then what am I doing? If I'm still just as angry, just as covetous or stingy, just as impatient or selfish as I was a few years ago, then I must ask, "Am I truly a believer? Is the Holy Spirit truly alive in me?"

The point is this journey to something more requires constant change. If we think it's okay to arrive at some point and then just stop, we're fooling ourselves. God has something amazing for us. He is in a continual process of redeeming us. He desires to free us from sinful patterns and attitudes that keep us stuck in our old and empty lives. He wants us to put on new attitudes and behaviors that bring greater purpose and meaning to our lives and a peace and joy that is beyond even what we've known with Him before. Do you see the difference? God's intention is not just that I have something more than I had before I met Him; He wants me to experience something more than what I experienced with Him last year!

I must view my life as a continual restoration project where He is making me over to what I was originally designed to be. If I could summarize the "life in process" attitude in one word it would be *humility*. As I've grown in my faith, I keep bumping up against this wall of pride. I used to think pride was just a cocky, braggadocious, stuck-up attitude. I've since come to realize that pride shows itself in many forms: defensiveness, selfishness, unwillingness to change, and desiring to do things for ourselves, to name a few. Humility sees life as a gift to be treasured and stewarded. Humility is teachable and willing to see life as a process of growth that never ends.

SUMMING IT UP

1. Christ died for us while we were still sinners. God loves us "as is," offering salvation as a free gift.

2. Salvation is not an excuse to remain "as is." To begin a journey toward something more, we must embrace the attitude that life is a process.

3. In a life in process, movement is normative, reflection is regular, and change is constant.

CHAPTER 2

A TASTE FOR MORE:
Let God Feed Your Soul

When people taste my wife's cooking, they ask me why I don't weigh 400 pounds. She's not only an amazing cook, she's a professional caterer with her own company. So on the few occasions when I want to give her a break or serve her, I am a little intimidated to cook a meal. I mean, when you're cooking for a caterer you can't throw a frozen pizza in the oven or try to pass off takeout food as your own. You've got to commit to the real deal.

One meal I can cook is chicken parmesan. The way I prepare it is to boil water for pasta and begin warming a jar of red sauce. Then I cut chicken, dip the pieces in egg, roll them in bread crumbs, and fry them in a pan with olive oil. I like to chop up fresh garlic and sprinkle some on the chicken after I flip the pieces. When they're close to done, I spoon on some red sauce, add some grated mozzarella, and cover the pan. Magnifico!

Now don't worry. This book hasn't turned into a cookbook for husbands of caterers. I merely want to turn our attention to what goes into a good meal: multiple ingredients, patience, timing, and a little skill. Preparing a good meal costs some of your time and energy, and it's not something you can mail in. In the same way, I want us to think about what it takes to truly feed our hungry souls.

SOUL HUNGER

We've become a culture driven by emotion, especially the desire for happiness. For many of us, emotional impulses are stronger than commitments, deeper than family bonds, and more powerful than logic. The search for the holy grail of happiness lures some of us away from our jobs, our marriages, and our homes.

> I believe God gave us emotions to drive us toward something more.

On the other hand, some of us are in the habit of suppressing our feelings, settling for a pale imitation of the life God desires for us. I frequently hear the expression "it is what it is" in response to a disappointing or frustrating situation. It's as if we're telling ourselves, "Suck it up. That's life." We think this attitude is virtuous, but stifling our emotions can be as unhealthy as overindulging them.

I believe God gave us emotions like unhappiness, boredom, and frustration to drive us toward something more. Just like physical hunger pangs tell us when we need to eat, these emotions signal that our souls need to be fed. Emotions of yearning, discontent, and frustration drive us to want to "fix" them. And the "fix" is not something to mask the emotion but to address what is underneath the emotion. So, the fact that God wired us to experience emotions, including negative emotions, is evidence that there *is* something more and that we're meant to pursue it.

One of the primary distinctions between humans and the animal kingdom is that we long and wish for things in our lives. Matt Heard, in his book *Life with a Capital L*, says, "It's what makes you and me human. Longing. Desire. Ache. Yearning. Soul thirst. Heart hunger. Fashioning us in his image, God made us different from animals. Our longing for something greater than mere survival showcases that distinction." Our desire for something more is proof that we are created in the image of God and that His thumbprint is on us. My dog doesn't have aspirations and wishes. She doesn't wish to become a famous fetcher or the first dog in the Oval Office. She has the basic needs of food, water, and companionship, but she doesn't experience longing the way you and I do.

Contrary to what some religions teach, longing is not inherently negative. The problem is not our longings; the problem is our misguided attempts to satisfy them, or our willingness to live with unmet longings. We've settled for less than God made us for. We don't have to settle for "it is what it is" when we serve and follow a God who can do anything!

God wants to feed the hunger in our souls. I hope one of the things that drew you to this book is your awareness of the hunger inside you. Deep down, we all have an appetite for purpose, meaning, and joy. Paul David Tripp puts it this way in his book *Quest for More:*

> There is woven inside each of us a desire for something more—a craving to be part of something bigger, greater, and more profound than our relatively meaningless day-by-day existence. ... It is that feeling of being part of something significant, of your place and your part mattering. For a moment your life seems bigger than your life. This bigger thing yanks you out of bed in the morning, and sometimes the excitement of it all makes it hard to sleep. It makes

all of the little things that you have to do every day seem more satisfying and more important because they are now connected to something more than self-survival. You have experienced a bit of transcendence.[1]

Unfortunately, many followers of God have never experienced that transcendence. We may have been Christians for years, but the way we've been living our Christian lives has not brought the "moreness" we desire. We've learned to either accept or deny our hunger or we've gone looking outside of God to satisfy our longings, sampling various "foods" in hope that they will fill us.

SPIRITUAL JUNK FOOD

As a teenager, I was a sucker for a good buffet—"good" meaning "all-you-can-eat." (What's with those buffets where they weigh your plate and tell you how much you owe?) I loved being able to eat as much as I wanted of whatever I liked. My favorite was the Pizza Hut lunch buffet: all the pizza, breadsticks, and dessert pizza I cared to eat. Oh to be young again, with a speedy metabolism.

We all know that stuffing ourselves with pizza is unhealthy. Similarly, we may try to fill our spiritual hunger with obviously bad food. Some turn to substances like alcohol or drugs to bring pleasure or to take the edge off, masking the pain of their longing. Others turn to sex, pornography, and similar indulgences to create an escape or to provide the sense of love and worth that our souls crave. Like the greasy food at a pizza buffet, these things bring pleasure for a while but leave us feeling rotten and, eventually, emptier than when we began.

Most of us know that such things won't nourish us. But just as we're tempted to overeat at a buffet, we are tempted to fill ourselves with foods that clearly damage our souls.

But what about the less obvious bad foods? Growing up, I tried to feed my soul with the approval of others. I couldn't wait for my grandparents to visit so I could show them my latest trophy or report card. I learned early on that good performance brought me feelings of love and admiration (and an occasional $5 in a card). Approval became like a drug to me. Many of us learn that if we perform well in school or work, we get the affirmation or compensation we desire from others. But it never lasts, and soon we need our approval fix again. As a result some of us become workaholics, believing if we just had more money or climbed a little higher on the ladder, we'd be able to relax and take that vacation we've been talking about.

Vacation itself can be a less obvious bad food. Instead of a well-earned reward, a vacation can be an illusion of escape. Indeed, some of us feed on thoughts of escape, the idea that if we could just find the right exit we'd arrive at the land of our dreams. And some of us act out the delusion, abandoning our existing lives for greener pastures, only to discover that we're no happier when we arrive.

Even things that are healthy in appropriate portions can become "junk food" when we use them to fill a hunger they weren't meant to fill. For example, sex in the context of marriage, utilized in a holy and intentional way, is profoundly meaningful. But when we

> As our physical bodies have a physical appetite so our souls have an appetite as well.

depend on sex (or anything other than God) to fulfill us, we end up disillusioned, frustrated, and worse off than when we began. It's not that these things are wrong in themselves, but we are asking them to do something they were never intended to do.

The point is that just as our physical bodies have a physical appetite and with that appetite come opportunities and choices, so our souls have an appetite as well. Anything that creates a dependency on something other than God is "bad soul food." And yet, though they never completely fill us, we reach for these spiritual junk foods anytime we're hungry, bored, or depressed.

While not technically a food, soda is a great illustration of the effect of junk food and why it falls short. When I was growing up my mom would say, "No soda with your meal. I don't want you to fill up on that and not eat your food." (When I was first on my own as an adult, I would spoil my appetite on purpose just because I could. I know, I'm quite the rebel!) Soda doesn't nourish us, but the carbonation gives us the *feeling* of being full without the substance. Soda tastes great and may be fun to drink, but you can't survive on soda. Likewise, your soul can't survive on the spiritual junk food of life. Without real substance and meaning, there will be no lasting joy.

Many of us have learned this over time. Maybe we've come to realize that the thing we thought would be enough never is; there will always be a next thing. Or maybe we've learned the hard way through a fall-out, a breakdown, a burnout, or simply a failure to reach what we were hoping for. In the process, we come to see that spiritual junk food can't satisfy the hunger of our souls. Unfortunately some of us are not there yet. We may know better, yet without the right alternative we just keep returning to the junk. We keep trying, keep pushing, keep telling ourselves that this time it will be different; this time it will work! And some of us just read those last words and thought, "I'm the exception. He doesn't mean me. This might be 'junk food' for most people, but it isn't for me."

Or some of us read those words and thought, "That's not me. I'm a Christian. I'm a follower of Jesus. I go to church." But none of that makes us immune to the temptations of spiritual junk food. In fact, many of us need to search our souls and confess that we are using church attendance or Christianity to accomplish something it was never intended to do. Can church be like a drug? It can be if our morality or religious activity becomes our identity or defines our worth as a person. We need to admit that we are indeed using junk food to fill the hunger, telling ourselves like Eve in the Garden that it's "good for food, and ... a delight to the eyes" (Genesis 3:6).

The prophet Jeremiah observed the human tendency to settle for spiritual junk food, missing out on the something more that could fill our souls. He speaks to this in Jeremiah 2:13: "... [My] people have committed two evils: they have forsaken me, the fountain of living waters, and hewed out [or dug] cisterns for themselves, broken cisterns that can hold no water."

> "One who is full loathes honey, but to one who is hungry everything bitter is sweet."

What God is saying through Jeremiah is that as human beings we turn away from the One who can quench our hunger and thirst, seeking instead our own ways to deal with our appetite. All of our efforts are "broken cisterns" that can't truly satisfy us. They don't hold water and therefore are ineffective. We spend all this energy digging our own cisterns, ending up confused and frustrated when they don't hold the water we thought they would. Then we spend more energy analyzing and rebuilding broken cisterns, all the while ignoring the fountain of living waters that is within our grasp.

Proverbs 27:7 tells us, "One who is full loathes honey, but to one who is hungry everything bitter is sweet." Could it be that you and I aren't truly longing for God and His Word (the honey) because we're already full? This verse reminds us that when you fill up on junk food, the best food will be rejected. And when you stay spiritually hungry for too long, you're more susceptible to junk food. At either extreme, you and I will miss out on what God intends: the great tasting, healthy, and satisfying meal only He provides. Some of us may not know that we're missing it! By trying to fill up on the junk food of our world, we may even come to loathe the honey that God invites us to experience.

Before we go any further, why not pause to evaluate your own life? How have you been feeding your hunger? Are you truly hungry for the life God has for you or are you too busy trying to create your own life? Are you pigging out on the world's buffet while missing true spiritual food and the life it nourishes? I'm not sure why we do this, but we do. Maybe it feels easier? Maybe we think if we pursue worldly things we can control them, but we can't control God? Maybe we think junk food doesn't cost a lot, but if you've been alive for any length of time, you've likely already seen the fall-out of a life of spiritual junk food.

SPIRITUAL FAST FOOD

Fast food has become a norm in our culture. We're all in a rush and we all need to eat, so a quick stop at the drive-thru is a more frequent occurrence than most of would like to admit. A recent study reports that 20 percent of all American meals are eaten in the car. Families running their kids to sports practices and after-school activities eat more meals in their cars than at home. Busy executives grab a fast-food breakfast and a morning coffee on the way to their morning meetings. Twenty-somethings sit in drive-thru lines for their triple, two pump, skinny vanilla, extra shot lattes and wild blueberry muffins because who has time to actually go inside a restaurant anymore, let alone prepare their own food at home?

What is the appeal of fast food? Why has it become the go-to meal for so many? I think there are two main reasons: fast food doesn't cost a lot and it doesn't take much time. And let's be honest, these have become two of our top criteria for pretty much everything: how much will it cost me and how long will it take? We tend to run from long-term exercise programs, preferring a diet pill or a quick fix. We buy products that are on sale regardless of their quality or whether we need them because we can't pass up an easy way to save money. Fast food is the perfect symbol of the way we prefer to live in our consumeristic culture.

Unfortunately this same thinking carries over to our experience of God, and is one of the key reasons so many people miss out on something more. Some of us approach God and our relationship with Him like we do fast food. We live a version of Christianity that doesn't cost a lot and doesn't take much time. While that can give us a sense of being filled, it fails to deeply nourish. We can live on fast food for some time, but if it's all we know our health will suffer. As a result, today we see a generation of Christians who are not spiritually healthy and have never tasted the good steak (or fill in your favorite slow-cooked, high quality meal) that God has to offer. And even if they did, they might not recognize it for what it is! By reducing Christianity to a bunch of stuff we should know and a bunch of stuff we should do, we miss the heart of a relationship with the living God.

In the Old Testament, the Jewish people were required to make regular pilgrimages to Jerusalem. In Exodus 23:14-17 we see the call for these pilgrimages and the celebration of certain festivals. Psalms 120-134 record the songs that were sung on the journey, known as the "songs of ascension" (sung as the pilgrims ascended the road to the heights of Jerusalem). From Abraham to Moses to Elijah, God continually called His people forward to trust and journey with Him. And it's in this journey that we begin to discover some of the amazing alternatives to spiritual junk food or spiritual fast food. The Jewish pilgrimage was a regular practice that taught God's people several things:

1. To value God correctly. By traveling distances that took days of effort, the people demonstrated that the things of God took priority over more day-to-day concerns. Their actions said, "God, You are important to us." The same thing happens when you and I travel to visit family in a distant place. We say by our actions, "You matter to us."

2. To view the world as temporary. By leaving the comforts of home, they demonstrated faith in something beyond

earthly comfort. They expressed belief in something more than what we see here.

3. To bring the fruits of labor. The travelers brought the best of what they had accumulated as an offering to God. Thus, they connected their daily work to God and demonstrated their belief that God is worth the cost.

4. To worship. As they traveled, the pilgrims sang songs that proclaimed God's worth. And when they had arrived, they worshiped God at the appointed feasts.

The bottom line is these pilgrimages were often long, time-consuming journeys that cost a great deal, but those who understood the value of a relationship with God were willing to take the trip!

Jesus said a lot about what it means to follow Him. For example, as recorded in Mark 8:34-36, He said, "If anyone would come after me, let him deny himself and take up his cross and follow me. For whoever would save his life will lose it, but whoever loses his life for my sake and the gospel's will save it. For what does it profit a man to gain the whole world and forfeit his soul?" There's a genuineness to Jesus' words that you don't hear in many places. He makes it clear that following Him isn't fast or inexpensive. It requires our sacrifice, yet it gives true life. Unfortunately, we don't hear a lot about sacrificial faith in our churches and religious experiences. In these verses and throughout the Gospels, Jesus invites us into a different kind of faith than most of us know. He offers the kind of life we were made for—the kind of life we long for—if we are willing to deny ourselves.

One of the tricky things about denying ourselves is our

motive. There will be some who will say, "I serve at the church, so I don't need to give any money." Or others will say, "I give money, so I'm denying myself." The reality is to deny ourselves involves truly putting ourselves aside. It's not convenient; it requires sacrifice. It means I won't live to satisfy my own desires but pursue the will of God. If we deny ourselves we are putting Jesus first which means we're not "helping Him out" or "giving Him a tip"—we are investing in His kingdom and His work.

This isn't to say that our journey must be miserable and full of suffering. The point is, the something more we desire cannot be obtained cheaply or quickly. A fast-food mentality about our spiritual experience will hinder us from receiving the true, satisfying spiritual banquet God has prepared. We have to remember that our world system is broken, full of sin, and in desperate need of redemption. Trying to find God through worldly techniques and approaches is pointless. Rather, we must fight against the temptations of the evil one, the broken world, and our own flesh, just like if we were on a physical diet we'd need to fight the temptations of potato chips and chocolate cake. The great news on a spiritual level is that the war is already won. Jesus died, overcame sin and death, and is inviting us to the life we were made for. And with this life comes freedom.

The need: Spiritual Nourishment

The options	Spiritual Junk Food	Spiritual Fast Food	True Spiritual Food
What is it?	Any activity that gives us a sense of fulfillment/temporary satisfaction apart from God or that keeps us from pursuing God fully.	A version of Christianity that we create to be convenient, easy, self-focused, and without sacrifice.	A truly satisfying, meaningful, and helpful spiritual provision.
What does it give?	A false and temporary satisfaction.	The illusion that we're following Jesus and, from time to time, a "taste" of life with God.	Joy, meaning, and purpose regardless of our circumstances.
What does it lack?	It lacks substance and ultimately lacks the presence and pleasure of God.	Because it's not true faith, it lacks God's power, presence, and pleasure.	It lacks all the pollutants and counterfeits that harm or distract Christians.
Why does it fail?	We are using it, often sinfully, to control or mask our true longing for God.	It's not true Christianity.	It does not fail. Read on!

Before you put down this book and return to a life of spiritual junk food or fast food, let's look at some powerful Scriptures from the Old and New Testaments that remind us of the life that is possible when we commit to following Jesus.

You make known to me the path of life; in your presence there is fullness of joy; at your right hand are pleasures forevermore.
Psalm 16:11

For a day in your courts is better than a thousand elsewhere.
Psalm 84:10a

Enter by the narrow gate. For the gate is wide and the way is easy that leads to destruction, and those who enter by it are many. For the gate is narrow and the way is hard that leads to life, and those who find it are few.
Matthew 7:13-14

The thief comes only to steal and kill and destroy. I came that they may have life and have it abundantly.
John 10:10

Jesus said to them, I am the bread of life; whoever comes to me shall not hunger, and whoever believes in me shall never thirst.
John 6:35

Jesus answered her, "If you knew the gift of God, and who it is that is saying to you, 'Give me a drink,' you would have asked him, and he would have given you living water. ... whoever drinks of the water that I will give him will never be thirsty again. The water that I will give him will become in him a spring of water welling up to eternal life."
John 4:10,14

For the things that are seen are transient [or temporary], but the things that are unseen are eternal.
2 Corinthians 4:18b

The message is all over the Bible. Yes, there are easier pursuits. There are endeavors that cost less of our time and energy. There are activities that bring more immediate, though temporary, pleasure. But none of these things are truly life.

None of them nurture us toward what we were made for or provide what we long for more than anything else. Let's not settle for spiritual junk food or fast food when God offers us the Bread of Life and Living Water.

Notes
1. Paul David Tripp, *A Quest for More: Living for Something Bigger than You* (2007; Greensboro, NC: New Growth Press).

SUMMING IT UP

1. Just as physical hunger tells us when our bodies need nourishment, God gave us negative emotions to signal when our souls need to be fed.

2. We miss out on God's best when we feast on spiritual junk food, looking to anything other than God to fill our souls. Even good things can become junk foods when we expect them to meet needs they were never intended to meet.

3. Spiritual fast food is a false version of Christianity that doesn't cost much and doesn't require much time. It creates the sense of being filled, but it fails to nourish.

CHAPTER 3

A MORE AUTHENTIC CONNECTION:
Surrender the System

In our age of ever evolving gadgets and gizmos, one enduring piece of technology is the vending machine. They've been updated over the years, but the basic concept remains the same: Insert a form of payment, make a selection, and receive your soda or movie rental or train ticket.

Traditional vending machines put customized satisfaction at your fingertips. You select your favorite snack from an array of options, locate its letter and number, press "A7," and watch the little spiral spin and drop your Cheetos into the access tray. Of course, you have to get the machine to accept your money. With some machines, the dollar bill has to be close to perfect —no tears, few wrinkles, and positioned exactly the right way or you're out of luck. You insert the bill and it goes in halfway before the machine spits it back. You try again. If you get the angle just right and the bill goes all the way in, you feel a sense of triumph. You've been approved for a bag of chips!

But don't count your

> Many of us approach God like a vending machine. We think that if we learn the right formula, God will give us what we want.

Cheetos before they're in the hatch. Sometimes the spiral spins but your snack gets stuck. This might require rocking the machine, pushing it forward and backward at just the right rhythm to drop your chips into the bin. Either that or you need a monkey-armed friend to reach inside the machine and retrieve the item you want.

Many of us approach God like a vending machine. We think that if we learn the right formula, God will give us what we want. We press "A," which might be reading the Bible or attending church. And then we look for number 7, which could be serving at church, praying the perfect prayer, or getting enough people to pray for us. Then we wait, expecting God to deliver a relationship, money relief, or healing. When we don't get what we desire, we think, "God must not really love me. I did what He wanted, and He didn't deliver!" Or maybe we try shaking the machine. We work harder, get more people to pray, and do extra religious activity, thinking certainly God will notice us and do what we want. We may not acknowledge these thoughts, but they drive us into many right actions for wrong motives. It's not that reading the Bible, attending church, or praying are not good things. They are! But trying to create a system that can be "worked" is destructive when it comes to a relational being like God.

WORKING THE SYSTEM

From an early age, we learn to treat relationships as transactional systems. As kids we quickly discover just which buttons to push to convince our parents give us what we want. We might pit mom against dad to accomplish our goals. As teens we might play the popularity game, where relationships with the right crowd are means to an end. This carries us into adulthood, where networking is encouraged and we trade favors with the expectation of getting something in return. In marriage, we learn to navigate around our spouses or to do certain things to put them in a good mood.

We substitute relationships for systems because systems can be manipulated, while relationships can be messy. People can disagree with us. By systematizing our relationships, we think that we can manage them, control them, and eliminate uncertainty. The scary thing is those who live this way actually think they're in relationships, but they're not; they are only manipulating systems. And they're missing the whole experience. They don't know what it is to be loved or even to be known, and so they often feel alone even among family and friends.

We're loneliest of all when we substitute a system for a relationship with God. I remember when I was in high school wanting desperately to date a girl who was popular and beautiful. I prayed every day and tried so hard to a perfect Christian in hope that God would hear my cries and give me a chance with her (and then of course my natural charm would take over). After about a year, when the girl said "yes," I thought I'd figured out God. My system had worked.

Ironically, that very relationship ended up pulling me away from God. She became the priority and God became my errand boy. I wouldn't have said that out loud, but it's how I acted. I worked at Burger King at the time and she worked at McDonalds, but fast food's Montagues and Capulets were not going to hold back true love! Or so I thought, until she dumped me for the fry guy and I was devastated. And so back to God I ran, this time asking for healing of a broken heart.

It would be so easy to write off this episode as teenage ignorance. But I repeated this pattern again and again. Different circumstances, but the same approach to God, with the same expectation that if I applied the right formula, pulled the right knobs on the God vending machine, I would get the goody I wanted.

I think many of us fall into the pattern I did of trying to use spiritual practices to get our way with God. If we're honest, we have to admit we've tried to work the system more than a few times. But when we reduce God to a system, we are reduced to lonely, disconnected people fending for ourselves in a challenging world. We are not experiencing relationship. We are merely pursuing a transaction that we think will benefit us.

But God will not be manipulated or controlled. By approaching God as a system, we miss who God really is. In a real relationship, the other person must be able to contradict you. If your "god" always agrees with your point of view and accommodates all your desires (even if you first have to jump through hoops), you don't have a relationship; you have a god in your own image. Sadly, I see this often in churches and among sincere Christians. We make the Bible say things it doesn't or we simply ignore the Scriptures we disagree with. Rather than knowing and relating with the God of the universe, we create a system called "god" that we can manage and control. The true, living God is not in our lives.

In Revelation 2, we read about the church in Ephesus. While we're not given motives for their actions and can't say for certain they were approaching God as a system, look at what Jesus says to them: "'I know your works, your toil and your patient endurance, and how you cannot bear with those who are evil, but have tested those who call themselves apostles and are not, and found them to be false. I know you are enduring patiently and bearing up for my name's sake, and you have not grown weary. But I have this against you, that you have abandoned the love you had at first."

This is a strong indictment, especially when you consider that most of us would be excited to attend a church that was doing what the Ephesians were doing. Jesus, however, had a very serious issue with them, and it had to do with their hearts. They had abandoned the love they had at first. While they were doing the right things, it seems they had drifted from a close, personal, even intimate relationship with God. Again, we don't know if they were doing all that they did to get something from God, but we know that they lost some of the relational dynamic. And I've seen from experience, when you keep doing the right things without the right heart, your good works quickly become empty and weak.

SETTLING FOR SECONDHAND

Let's return to our vending machine analogy. Another feature of vending machines is the layer of glass that separates us from what's inside. We'll never have firsthand contact with most of the machine's contents. We are on the wrong side of the glass for that. Our experience is removed, separated. It's second-hand.

In fact, much of contemporary life is restricted to secondhand experience. Consider television. Every time you watch TV you see people doing more exciting things than you are doing. I mean you never see a guy slumped on a couch with popcorn and potato chip crumbs all over his shirt, right? On television, people travel to exotic locations, solve crimes, drive fast cars, and come up with more hilarious one-liners than a stand-up comedian. (Sorry, no one is that funny in real life!) These scenes draw us in so that we feel like we are experiencing them too. But we aren't. We are on the wrong side of the glass.

Video games are built on the same premise. Sure, they give you a sense of real action but they are anything but real. Have you ever watched someone play a video game? They bob and weave, trying to avoid getting hit. Hey, reality check. It's just a game! Since they're on the wrong side of the glass, their experience is only second-hand.

I wonder if God is inviting us to the other side of the glass, spiritually speaking. We settle for secondhand faith experiences, elevating pastors and missionaries and applauding people who volunteer in ministry. We create categories of "super Christians," and we love hearing about what God is doing through them. We imagine ourselves impacting others like these heroes of the church do. We attend church services and watch the worship team, listen to the preacher, and get a sense that their faith experience is ours. We are inspired by their passion and almost believe it's *our* passion. But sadly it's just another secondhand experience, dimly observed from the wrong side of the glass. Is this what we're willing to settle for?

Beginning in Genesis 25, the Bible provides an example of someone who moved from a secondhand to a firsthand encounter with God. Jacob, whose name means "deceiver" or "heel grabber," was born gripping the heel of his brother. He lived up to his name on a number of occasions. With his mother's help, he dressed as his brother to trick his nearly blind father into giving him the family blessing. Later in life he deceived his father-in-law, Laban, by sorting herds of animals in his own favor to increase his wealth at his father-in-law's expense.

Jacob was part of a spiritual family, called by God for a special assignment. He grew up around religious practices and learned what was expected of him. While he verbally affirmed religious traditions and participated in religious practices, he found ways to leverage them for his purposes. Jacob was a key biblical figure, and yet I wonder how much of his life was truly connected to God in a personal way. From an outside perspective, it sure seems like he surrounded himself with all the right things yet experienced faith vicariously through others. It seems he lived his spiritual life on the wrong side of the glass.

Jacob demonstrates that when we relate to God from a secondhand position, we tend not to trust God because we don't really know Him. From secondhand, God is not someone to trust, let alone love. He is someone to negotiate with, warily, to be sure we are not taken advantage of. The relationship is transactional: we give God something (acknowledgement, worship, religious works), and in exchange He must give us what we want (contentment, status, entry to heaven). We arrange our own blessings, looking to take care of ourselves. We tend to be self-focused, always worried about how things will impact us. We become fearful and anxious, even a little paranoid because all of life is on our shoulders.

> Allowing Him into the depths of our lives sometimes means we must wrestle with God.

Disconnected from the true God, we struggle with personal relationships. All of these issues plagued Jacob for many years.

Then comes Genesis 32, the story of Jacob wrestling with God. I'm not sure if Jacob understands the significance immediately, but by the end of the battle it's clear. Maybe for the first time in his life, he's gotten up close and personal with God, hand to hand and face to face. God ceases to be the "God of my fathers" and becomes "my God."

Like Jacob, some of us have kept God at arm's length. But allowing Him into the depths of our lives sometimes means we must wrestle with God. At one point in Jacob's encounter, God (in the form of a mysterious stranger) touches Jacob's hip and puts it out of joint. I think this is the moment when Jacob realizes that the stranger is God. Jacob recognizes the bigness of God and how easily He could defeat Jacob if He wanted to. I think Jacob ceases wrestling at this point and is just holding on. Similarly, we can lose sight of how big God really is and not fully trust Him with the important stuff in life. But when we move to a firsthand experience of God, we learn to trust Him because we've seen Him up close. Jacob hangs onto God, and God chooses to bless Him and redefine His identity.

I know many of us have baggage that makes us feel like our efforts at faith haven't worked. I realize that it feels safer to live vicariously through others. But aside from missing the best of what God intends for us, a secondhand faith is also easy to abandon. At best, we coast along without growth and become bored. Or worse, we criticize and complain and learn to play both sides. Jacob had a great faith heritage and lived among godly people, but he was trusting in himself and managing his own success. While on the surface it looked like he was succeeding, he was missing out on God's best and God's way.

When we approach God as a system or settle for a secondhand experience of Him, we will never become the people we were designed to be. We will never know the living God. If we maintain an image of Him at all, it will be an impotent, distant, and empty image. In order to know God and to experience what He has in store for our lives, we must stop pressing buttons in a vain attempt to manipulate and move to the other side of the glass. We must abandon transactional spirituality and get personal and relational.

THE REAL DEAL

The Bible is full of evidence that we're made for personal relationship with God. In Genesis 3, we see a God who enjoys going on walks with Adam and Eve and who pursues them out of love and concern. Abraham is called to be the father of a "people" of God. Moses has the privilege of talking and meeting with God (Exodus 33). The prophets are God's personal ambassadors, calling the nation to a covenant-keeping God who loves them and longs to draw them near. The Psalms are probably the best Old Testament example of the personal relationship we are intended to have with God. They are filled with authentic cries to God and affirmations of God's love for His people. If you haven't read them in a while, I recommend setting aside time to read a Psalm every day for a deeper sense of what it means to know God personally.

Let's look at just two of the Psalms that can help us understand this issue of personal connection: Psalm 16 and Psalm 23. I referenced Psalm 16 in the previous chapter, but let's dig a little deeper. The first two verses state, "Preserve me, O God, for in you I take refuge. I say to the Lᴏʀᴅ, 'You are my Lord; I have no good apart from you.'" The Psalmist does not regard God as a vending machine or approach God through a transactional system. Instead he says, "God, you are a place of rest. Being with you is restorative to me. The good stuff in life is found in You!" Here's a guy who's discovered the something more that we all long for, and he's found it in a personal relationship with God.

> A relationship with God calms and restores our noisy souls, bringing peace where there is worry and longing.

The Psalm goes on to demonstrate the pain and difficultly we experience when we try to find life outside of God. Then in verses 7-8, the Psalmist states, "I bless the Lᴏʀᴅ who gives me counsel; in the night also my heart instructs me. I have set the Lᴏʀᴅ always before me; because he is at my right hand, I shall not be shaken." When we foster a first-hand, up close and personal, inside the glass kind of connection with God, we find regular counsel, direction, and confidence to face whatever life throws at us. While this Psalm does not direct us on how to build this kind of connection, it's clear that the Psalmist has grown close enough to God to break through rituals and systems. He has found life, security, and meaning in a personal first-hand relationship with God.

Psalm 23 is similar. Its familiarity may cause us to overlook the relational significance of its content. The Psalm begins, "The Lᴏʀᴅ is my shepherd; I shall not want. He makes me lie down in green pastures. He leads me beside still waters. He restores my soul." It's a comforting image, which is why this Psalm is often read at funerals, but don't miss what the Psalmist is saying: A relationship with God calms and restores our noisy souls, bringing peace where there is worry and longing. The astonishing impact of that kind of connection is evident in verse 4: "Even though I walk through the valley of the shadow of death, I will fear no evil, for you are with me."

I memorized these words as a child, but I'm only now beginning to grasp their significance. Something more is not just about joy and passion but also about peace and contentment. When we truly know God, it changes our outlook on life. It changes where we find joy and what concerns us. We discover a solid place to rest amidst the storms and constant motion of our world. When we settle for a distant, removed, impersonal connection with God, not only will we look for happiness in all the wrong places but we'll miss out on the security and rest that we so need in our hyperactive lives and broken world.

A personal connection with God is seen in the New Testament as well. By sending Jesus to earth, God demonstrated the desire to meet us face to face. The Gospels of Matthew, Mark, Luke, and John reveal an eagerly relational God through the person of Jesus. One of my favorite stories appears in John 3, where a religious leader by the name of Nicodemus comes to see Jesus at night. Nicodemus was a Pharisee who knew and taught the religious law and probably even led worship services. He appeared to be right with God, but he was missing a personal connection because of his "box."

We all carry a box, a perspective in which we try to contain God. Nicodemus was trying to put God in the box of religious practice and law. But Jesus' words in verse 3 break through the box: "Truly, truly, I say to you, unless one is born again he cannot see the kingdom of God." It's as if Jesus is saying, "Nicodemus, what you need is not something to add to what you already know. It's not a new formula for your system. It's not another asset you can use in a transaction with God. The life that you long for requires a transformation, not an addition!"

If you and I seek something more in a new trend or a new process without changing our fundamental connection with God, we won't find it. Something more requires not a spiritual makeover, a reboot, or an upgrade. Something more requires a complete transformation. One of the reasons I missed God as a young adult was that my life, even as a Christian, was about performance, achievement, and figuring out what worked. But here, through his conversation with Nicodemus, Jesus tells us that we need a whole new life. Instead of trying to manipulate God with our process, we must be changed by God, and relate to Him as a loving parent and not a machine.

Let's look at one more Scripture before moving on to some suggestions for deepening a relationship with God. The book of Hebrews is an amazing treatise on who Jesus is and how He fulfills the aspirations and promises of the Old Testament (an old system). The book explains how, through Jesus, we can come closer to God than ever before. Hebrews 10, beginning in verse 19, states, "... since we have confidence to enter the holy places by the blood of Jesus, by the new and living way that he opened for us ... let us *draw near* with a true heart in full assurance of faith" (emphasis added). Don't miss what God is saying: He wants us to be close to Him. We don't need to fear His rejection or doubt His intentions. We don't need to manipulate or control. We simply need to present ourselves, yield, and relate.

So what does that look like? Answering that question is a bit like telling someone how to be in love. You can describe what a person in love acts like – what they tend to think about and do. You can explain that a guy in love might bring his girl flowers. You can explain that a girl may make several calls or show up where her guy is. But can you explain how to be in love? I don't think you can. There's nothing wrong with flowers or phone calls, but they can become an empty gesture or ritual if they're not from the heart. Similarly, I caution you against adopting the following suggestions as currency for your vending machine. I offer these suggestions with a reminder to emphasize heart change over step-by-step actions:

1. Get gut-level honest about how you've viewed God and your interactions with Him.

For me, getting honest with God hasn't been a one-time event but a process. That process has led me to confess many times how I've tried to use God to get my way. I've had to admit that when my life is going well, I tend to forget my need for God. I've confessed that I like God when He agrees with me, but I'm not so eager to do things His way when I don't agree. I've been angry when it felt like God would do what I thought He should do, and then He didn't. I've been resentful when I felt like I was promised or entitled to something, and God didn't come through. As with Jacob, these occasions have involved wrestling, yelling at God, working it out. Sometimes it can be as simple as, "God, I'm angry and totally frustrated with you!" or "God, I'm not feeling close to you. Actually I've become bored with you."

The bottom line is you need to be real about your relationship with God. A heart stays hardened only when it doesn't know that it's hardened. Being honest with God, starting with a gut-level inventory, is a great way to foster the kind of personal connection you'll need for a something more journey. This inventory may require more than one conversation with God and, depending on how you are used to relating to God, may be quite challenging. The great thing is God already knows where we are. He knows our thoughts and our hearts. We may think we're hiding our true selves, but nothing is hidden from God. He's waiting for us to be honest about what He already knows.

2. Remember where you've come from.

Nicodemus didn't realize he needed to be born again. But without rebirth, his religion was meaningless and he was lost. If you're a Christian, there was a time when you were dead in your sin. But your faith in Jesus' death and resurrection changed your identity and destiny. If we forget how lost we were—utterly desperate and without hope—we can begin to believe that we're redeeming ourselves. We can focus on becoming good people and miss how utterly sinful we are apart from Jesus.

> Getting personal with God requires creating space and time for a close relationship.

Remembering what you've been saved from will rekindle a gratitude and passion for the God who rescued you.

We've all heard stories of celebrities who grew up in poverty, became rich, and then forgot where they came from.

They've abandoned friendships and stopped being grateful. They've become entitled and arrogant. Unfortunately, I've met some Christians who've forgotten where they came from. They've become judgmental, looking down on messy people and refusing to offer grace to anyone. If you forget your desperate need for God's grace, you will not have grace for others and will not have a close relationship with God. Jesus reserved his harshest words for people like the Pharisees who failed to see their own need. Remembering our need and God's amazing grace takes us closer to the life we were made to live.

3. Create space for your relationship with God.

When I do marriage counseling, I often hear, "The spark is gone. How do we get it back?" The couple looks to me for some magic that will erase years of neglect and conflict. There is no such magic, but what I often encourage Is to schedule a regular date night. Is the date night guaranteed to renew the spark? No. Renewed intimacy often requires learning new patterns, uncovering unresolved conflict, and other serious heart work. However, if we don't create space and time for each other, it's pretty much a guarantee that the spark *won't* return. It's not that the date night is magical. It simply creates space for intimacy. Similarly, getting personal with God requires creating space and time for a close relationship. There is no magic wand or quick fix. It is remedial spiritual work, not on God's part but on ours.

Building any relationship requires communication, both speaking and listening. In a relationship with God, this means time in the Bible and time in prayer. This is probably not new to you, but relational Scripture reading and prayer can be challenging if you've been treating these things as buttons on a vending machine. Or maybe they've become empty practices performed as an obligation.

To recapture a relational perspective, we must read the Bible as if hearing the very words of God. I've had to get creative with this because of my former tendency to systematize. I have had seasons of meditating on individual verses and seasons of journaling on passages of Scripture. Sometimes I select a book of the Bible and read the same section every day for a month. The key is not the activity but my perspective. I must view time with the Bible as an ongoing conversation with God. It's God joining me for a cup of coffee and sharing His heart. I listen and share my own. It's God sitting beside me on the porch telling stories of real people who wrestled with the same issues I face. It's God sitting across from me in the counseling office providing direction for my next few steps. I've found that the more I hear and process the words of God in the Bible, the better I understand His heart and trust His ways.

Prayer is an opportunity for personal processing. When I pray, I try to share with God all of who I am. God knows it all anyway; if I cannot share all of myself with Him in prayer I am truly lost. So I take time to reflect, asking God to search me and know me. When I am fearful or angry, I seek to uncover the source, uncovering and exploring and confessing the deeper issues of my heart. I also prioritize praying for others. If I'm not careful, prayer can become a laundry list of the things I need God to do for me, as if He were my heavenly errand boy. Rather, I must share my heart, submit my plans, and surrender myself.

When I pray for others, truly bringing them before God, I find that I become less selfish. By the time I get to my concerns, I'm in a better state of mind to truly relate with God. The tried and true acronym of ACTS—Adoration, Confession, Thanksgiving, and Supplication—can help foster relational prayer, if you fight the tendency to make it yet another formula. You may also want to pay attention to your surroundings. For example, I enjoy praying and meditating on Scripture while at a park, on a walk, or anywhere outside.

I love Brennan Manning's thoughts on Bible reading and prayer in *The Ragamuffin Gospel*:

> The Word we study has to be the Word we pray. My personal experience of the relentless tenderness of God came not from exegetes, theologians, and spiritual writers, but from sitting still in the presence of the living Word and beseeching Him to help me understand with my head and heart His written Word. Sheer scholarship alone cannot reveal to us the gospel of grace. We must never allow the authority of books, institutions, or leaders to replace the authority of *knowing* Jesus Christ personally and directly. When the religious views of others interpose between us and the primary experience of Jesus as the Christ, we become unconvicted and unpersuasive travel agents handing out brochures to places we have never visited.[1]

I admit that as a Christian and even as a pastor I have been guilty of handing out brochures to places I haven't visited. Because I didn't fully understand what it meant to get personal with God, I was missing a fundamental piece of what it means to be a Christian. While I wasn't consciously faking it, I was telling people about something I had yet to experience. Now that I've been traveling this relational road for a while, I never want to go back. I only want to know Jesus more.

Notes

1. Brennan Manning, *The Ragamuffin Gospel: Good News for the Bedraggled, Beat-Up, and Burnt Out* (2005; Colorado Springs: Multnomah).

SUMMING IT UP

1. If we approach God through a system or settle for a secondhand experience of Him, we will never know the true and living God.

2. A personal connection with God requires a heart-level transformation.

3. To foster intimacy with God, get honest about how you've viewed Him, remember where you've come from, and create space for a relationship with Him.

CHAPTER 4

MORE FOCUS:
Be Intentional

As a youth pastor working for 14 years, I had more than my share of all-nighters. At one overnight event, I developed a game to help my students understand what it takes to move forward in life and ministry. I called it "Mayhem." I rummaged through the closets of the church and found a couple of balls, a sand shovel, a hula hoop, and a few other objects. I divided the students into two teams of about 25 each and gave each team a collection of objects. I instructed them, "The goal of Mayhem is to win the game by scoring the most points, and you need to figure out how to score points. I'm not going to tell you. Ready? Go!"

Without any other direction, a few kids started to throw balls at the other team. I ran over to one of the throwers and called him out. Then I ran to another kid who got hit and called him out. One girl started hula hooping, and I gave her 1,000 points. When someone else hula hooped, I called her out and deducted 150 points from her team's score, which I wasn't even keeping track of. For the next ten minutes I continued to change the rules, randomly award points, call people out, or even kick some people entirely out of the game, all without explaining my actions. Eventually, one by one the kids started sitting down, walking away, and refusing to play. They called

Mayhem "the worst game ever!" Why? Because lots of activity with no purpose is pointless!

So far we've discussed the heart changes required to move toward something more. In Chapter 1 we saw that mindset is critical. If we try to put new practices in place without changing our perspective, we will eventually be disappointed by yet one more failed attempt at discovering the life God has for us. We must start with the

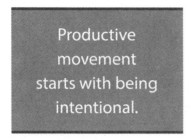

Productive movement starts with being intentional.

attitude that life is about process and that we're engaging in a journey, not an event. In Chapter 2, we examined how the spiritual junk foods and fast foods we feed our souls fall far short of God's intention. But if we settle for less, not realizing what's at stake, we won't be motivated to take the next step.

In Chapter 3, we saw that the key is to understand our connection with God as a relationship. This isn't new information, but I've found if we examine our lives more closely, most of us will realize that much of our connection with God is about anything but relationship. When I start to engage with God from a relational vantage point, I begin to see just how much He really does love me and desire good things for me. We ended Chapter 3 discussing a few ideas for movement. The remainder of the book will get practical on the activities and environment that characterize the kind of life we were made to live.

ACTIVITY WITH PURPOSE

Productive movement starts with being intentional. Being intentional doesn't just mean having good intentions. How many of us have fallen for this one? We listen to a sermon, read a book, or talk with a counselor and we feel convicted, motivated, maybe even a little guilty about what we haven't been doing. And we mistake that feeling for action. I spoke with a married couple a few weeks after a sermon I preached on marriage. The husband said, "That was a great sermon, Pastor. Our marriage needs help, and I know it's going to get better now." I replied, "Great! So what are you *doing* differently?" The husband met my question with a blank stare, as if to say, "Doing? I feel really bad about my marriage. Isn't that enough?"

I have often been guilty of this in my relationship with God. I mistake feelings, good intentions, and desires for actually doing something. But those are two very different things! Now obviously you can start *doing* a lot of activity and fall right back into a system or manipulative pattern with God. We started this book discussing mindset and heart, and I don't want you to miss that as we go forward.

We've seen that being intentional is different from having good intentions, but it's not *just* activity. Being intentional is activity with a purpose. Many of us mistake activity for progress. I see this in the church all the time. There are churches that keep Christians busy with lots of activity yet have little spiritual progress or effectiveness to show for it. The thinking is, "We're doing all this stuff, so I'm sure something good is happening!" When churches fail to ask questions like *Why?* or *Where is this taking people?*, they become bloated with a buffet of programs that keep people involved but don't actually transform lives.

As individuals, we fall prey to this in our busy lives. We're constantly moving and doing yet rarely pause to ask, "Where are we going? And do I even want to go there?" My wife and

I recently had this realization. We have three kids, she has her own business, and I pastor a church. There is constant movement in our home. And over the last few years we've both become aware of the gnawing, nagging feeling that we're missing it. We couldn't even put words to what we are missing, but we felt a lack depth or meaning. It wasn't until we spent two months in Florida on a sabbatical—an intentional time away from ministry—that things really clicked. We realized that we've been living reactive rather than proactive lives. We've been responding to what is coming at us instead of getting on top of it and being intentional. The scary truth we recognized is that someone else—in fact lots of someones, though they meant no harm—were actually controlling our lives while we were just trying to stay above water.

We understood anew that as parents we must ask ourselves: Who do we want to be? What do we want our kids to value? What is truly important to us? What do we want our family to be known for? If we never stop to consider such questions, we will succumb to our culture. We'll end up surviving parenthood but wondering why our kids are off in all directions with little purpose and no godly foundation.

> Commitment and diligence, regardless of feelings, is an important character trait.

Similarly in our faith lives, we may find that we are doing spiritual activity without a clear understanding of its purpose. We go to church, maybe even read the Bible and pray, but we see those activities as an end to themselves. We give ourselves accolades for completing the task instead of pursuing its purpose in our lives. Growing up in a Christian home, I found myself falling into this pattern. I considered myself a good Christian when I read my Bible or attended a religious event, but I was secretly empty, wondering why my faith was stagnant. As I faithfully read the Bible, I wondered why I wasn't experiencing what people in the Bible experienced.

Now I'm not saying there aren't times when I just read the Bible or show up at church because I know it's good for me, even though I'm not "feeling" it. Sometimes that is needed. Commitment and diligence, regardless of feelings, is an important character trait. My point is never to confuse the activity with the purpose. As Dawson Trotman, founder of the Navigators, famously said, "Emotion is no substitute for action, action is no substitute for production, and production is no substitute for reproduction." Spiritual disciplines, as they're often called, are tools to strengthen our relationship, growth, and connection with God. But they are not the *same thing* as relationship, growth, or connection. They are tools, but they are not the purpose.

Sometimes in a discussion like this, we Christians get a little uncomfortable. We say things like, "Our faith comes only by God's grace." We imply that we don't need to *do* anything because that would be trying to earn God's favor and there's nothing we can do to earn God's love. But such thinking is an over-simplification and misunderstanding of biblical texts. James 2:17 reminds us that faith without works is dead faith. True faith is active. True growth must be a cooperation of our intentional action and God's spiritual transformation. It's not an either-or venture.

I missed this so often in my younger years as a Christian.

Spiritual activities are intended to help us grow, not to improve our standing with God or to win us His love or approval. His love for us is purely by grace, our salvation in Christ a gift that can't be earned. Our transformation and sanctification are works of God's Spirit, but just sitting and waiting for them to happen is not God's intention, as we'll see in the next section.

It always comes back to the heart. If we're trying to get in good with God, we will do the right things from the wrong heart. If we use the disciplines He gives us as tools for our growth, we are cooperating with His plan and will experience the life we were made to experience because we are doing the right things in the right way from the right heart.

INTENTIONAL GODLINESS

If being intentional is activity with a purpose, how does intentional living contribute to our quest for something more? Embracing and engaging in the life God has for us doesn't just happen if we passively wait for it. To better understand this, let's look at the Apostle Paul's words to Timothy, his pastoral protégé. Paul writes in 1 Timothy 4:6-10:

> If you point these things out to the brothers and sisters, you will be a good minister of Christ Jesus, nourished on the truths of the faith and of the good teaching that you have followed. Have nothing to do with godless myths and old wives' tales; rather, train yourself to be godly. For physical training is of some value, but godliness has value for all things, holding promise for both the present life and the life to come. This is a trustworthy saying that deserves full acceptance. That is why we labor and strive, because we

have put our hope in the living God, who is the Savior of all people, and especially of those who believe.

Paul is concerned about the rampant false teaching that is all around this young church. While the flavors of false teaching may be different from what are popular today, Paul's instructions remain powerful. In fact, I believe we can apply these truths to our discussion of intentional movement. Consider what Paul has to say about the intentional pursuit of godly living.

1. Godly living requires training.

In verses 7 and 8, Paul compares the pursuit of godliness to physical training of a very active and strenuous sort. On many occasions I've wanted to lose weight. In order to accomplish that goal I needed to change my eating habits, get up earlier, and actually exercise. These actions are not convenient, quick, or easy, but they are the only way to make change happen.

The same is true of our spiritual lives. Yes, it is God who transforms us, but He accomplishes this change through a partnership between our efforts and His Spirit. If we emphasize the role of one to the detriment of the other, we miss God's plan. Paul uses the Greek

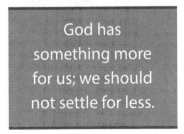

God has something more for us; we should not settle for less.

word *gymnazo*, which shares a root with our word gymnasium. The translated word *training* involves activity, exercise, commitments, discipline, and ongoing choices. Words like *toil*, *strive*, *devote*, and *persist* are all associated with this concept. Take a moment to think deeply about physical training as a metaphor for spiritual growth, and you'll likely identify several intentional spiritual activities you can participate in right away. For example memorizing Scripture can be something that is done repetitively with additional "weight" (more verses) added to expand your understanding. Just as in training, you'll have short-term and long-term goals and activities you undertake to accomplish those goals.

2. Godly living requires the right focus.

Verses 8 through 10 make it clear that godliness isn't for self-gain or the approval of others. It's about a promise for life and a future. It's about hope in the living God and Savior. These are powerful motivators in light of the sacrifice and commitment required to grow. Again in the weight loss illustration, I won't exercise if there is no likelihood that I will get healthier and less heavy. As I tell people, "I only run when I'm being chased!" This is my way of saying that I don't exercise for fun.

God has something more for us; we should not settle for less. Pastor and author Bill Hybels defines vision as "a picture of the future that produces passion." When we have a clear vision of who God made us to be, we will run hard to make it become a reality. And don't underestimate the importance of a mental image. If you're not clear what a godly person looks like, you won't know what you're running towards, or when you get there.

The Bible has many of descriptions of godliness. It wouldn't be a bad idea to jot these down as you discover them. The fruit of the Spirit in Galatians 5:22-23 and the "love" chapter, 1 Corinthians 13, are two places to find lists of godly qualities. But one of the best ways to see God's intention for humanity is to study the life of Jesus. In Jesus we see the character and actions of a human being fully surrendered to God and living a life of meaning, purpose, and joy. A clear vision of a life that reflects Jesus inspires the action required for growth.

3. Godly living requires community.

In order to examine this concept, we need to read a little further in our text. Here's 1 Timothy 4:12-16:

> Don't let anyone look down on you because you are young, but set an example for the believers in speech, in conduct, in love, in faith and in purity. Until I come, devote yourself to the public reading of Scripture, to preaching and to teaching. Do not neglect your gift, which was given you through prophecy when the body of elders laid their hands on you. Be diligent in these matters; give yourself wholly to them, so that everyone may see your progress. Watch your life and doctrine closely. Persevere in them, because if you do, you will save both yourself and your hearers.

I don't know about you, but I've found it pretty easy to love others when there's no one there! I can envision how loving and kind I would be, but without people in the equation I have no opportunity to practice and work out my salvation. Godly living can be done only in community. Timothy was the pastor of a church, a community of faith. And Paul called Timothy to set the example. Like Timothy and his fellow believers, we are to be active enough in each other's lives that we can call each other forward through example and mutual encouragement. We will talk more about this in the next chapter and throughout the book because community is an essential—and often overlooked—element of something more for all Christians in every church. For now, understand that intentional, true spiritual growth toward godliness doesn't happen in isolation. We need one another.

4. Godly living impacts more than just you.

This principle grows out of the previous one. The benefits of living for something more extend far beyond ourselves and our individual transformation. In verse 16, Paul calls Timothy to persevere in his training because his growth toward godliness positively impacts others. People like your spouse, your family, your friends, and your church will all be impacted by your growth and godly living, as you will by theirs. I love how Hudson Taylor, the trailblazing missionary to China, said it: "If your father and mother, your sister and brother, if the very cat and dog in the house are not the better and happier for your being a Christian, it is a question whether you really are one." (Man, I think I owe my dog an apology or two!)

Paul encourages Timothy in verse 15 to let everyone see his progress. Why would Paul mention this? Isn't this grandstanding? No. Maybe it has to do with accountability. Maybe it's a matter of mutual encouragement. Maybe Paul believes that every church needs growing, godly leaders. I'm guessing it's a combination of all of these things.

WIND AND SAILS

Spiritual growth and godliness don't just happen. In no way do I want to downplay the work of the Holy Spirit. The intentional activity I'm talking about includes things like surrender, specific confession, fasting, obedience, and submitting to God's authority in our lives. It is God who does the transformation through the indwelling Holy Spirit!

However, given our current evangelical culture's emphasis on grace (which I think is long overdue), we may inadvertently downplay our personal effort. Let me say it again: Spiritual growth is a partnership between God's Spirit and our efforts. My favorite illustration of this partnership, not original to me, is a sailboat. A sailboat depends on the wind to propel it forward, but a sail must be raised to catch the wind. The effort of raising the sail maximizes the wind's effect on the boat. Did the sail move the boat forward? No, the wind did. Was raising the sail unnecessary? Well, a wind may drive a boat with no sail, but not very far, not very fast, and not necessarily in the right direction. And it's more than just wind and sail. A skilled sailor, acting with intention, will maximize the power of the wind by setting the sails just so and carefully minding the tiller. The boat's movement toward the desired goal is a partnership between wind, sail, and sailor. This is the kind of partnership that moves us forward spiritually as well. It's not just activity. It's *intentional* spiritual activity!

Before we leave this chapter I want to share two resources that have helped me "adjust my sails." The first is a powerful chart from T. J. Addington's book *Leading from the Sandbox*. Addington defines intentional living as "the discipline of

> Every "yes" requires a "no" to something else, and often many somethings.

knowing how God made you, defining the top issues in your life and work, and executing with an intentional plan that connects your schedule with your priorities in a way that maximizes your God-given gifting and call." At the other end of the spectrum is what Addington calls "accidental living." Note the contrasts in Addington's chart:[1]

CONTINUUM:

Accidental Living	Intentional Living
* Lives moment by moment	* Lives within structure
* Often harried	* Seldom harried
* Little advance planning	* Significant advance planning
* Doesn't distinguish big and and small rocks	* Distinguishes critical/ non-critical
* Busy without well-defined priorities	* Schedule revolves around key priorities
* Allows life to determine schedule	* Mission drives schedule

Intentional movement will require some big decisions, advance planning, and prioritizing. I have no desire to scare you off, and maybe this is why we have an epidemic of spiritual shallowness in our culture. In my own life, a lot of this comes down to setting aside several hours every four to six months and mapping things out. Once I've devoted that time, it's just a matter of "working the plan."

The second resource is a principle I've been refining in my life, a freeing principle that has made all the difference in my intentionality. I call it "The Law of Yes." Simply stated, it's the recognition that every *yes* is also a *no*. Here's how it works: Every time I'm about to say yes to something, I stop and ask myself, "What would this require saying no to?" Every yes requires a no to something else, and often many somethings. Here's an obvious example. When I said yes to marrying Lisa, I was saying no to dating other women. Perhaps less obviously, when I say yes to more meetings and activities, I'm saying no to spending time with my daughters. And when I say yes to four once-a-month commitments, I've inadvertently said no to being home one evening a week. Some of those yeses may be necessary for my job or ministry; some of them might be critical to my growth. I'm not suggesting we stop saying yes. I'm urging you to be aware of what you are *choosing* when you say yes.

We live in a culture that constantly tries to buck the Law of Yes. We rack up large credit card bills because we refuse to say no or even to wait on something we want. We burn out physically because we say yes to every opportunity, and our unwillingness to say no has us running at an unsustainable pace. We are sapped emotionally because we continually expand our circle of care, never saying no, and end up feeling responsible for more people than any human being can adequately care for.

Bucking the Law of Yes won't cut it in our spiritual lives. Spiritual growth requires intentional yeses. If we're not willing to count the cost and be cognizant of the things we are also saying no to, we'll try to do it all and feel discouraged when we don't see spiritual progress in our lives. I can't lose weight and still say yes to ice cream and donuts. But if we know that we are making the best yes, be it spiritual growth or improved health, we are willing to accept the no's because we are confident the tradeoff is positive for what we intend. I've seen too many people who desire to grow but never take the Law of Yes into account. They find themselves back where we began this book, yearning for something more yet never seeming to find it.

Set aside a few hours. Assess where you are, who God made you to be, and where you want to be in the future. Identify some worthy spiritual goals. Paint a picture in your mind of what you'd like to become. Remember, a good vision is a picture of the future that produces passion! Then create a plan with simple steps and appropriate, attainable activities. Work the plan intentionally, saying yes to what you need and no to what you don't. Finally, build in a feedback loop every few months, a self-evaluation or a check-in with your spouse or partner or group to assess and adjust your plan. In this way, you'll move from good intentions to intentional growth.

Notes
1. T.J. Addington, *Leading from the Sandbox: How to Develop, Empower, and Release High-Impact Ministry Teams* (2010; Colorado Springs: NavPress).

SUMMING IT UP

1. Being intentional means more than having good intentions. It means engaging in activity with a purpose.

2. Intentional godliness requires training, focus, and community and results in something more for us and the people in our lives.

3. Spiritual growth is a partnership between God's Spirit and our effort. Resources like Addington's chart and the Law of Yes can make our efforts more intentional.

CHAPTER 5

MORE RELATIONSHIPS:
Create Community

When I was growing up there was a big emphasis on your "personal relationship" with Jesus. Speakers would say, "Going to church doesn't make you a Christian just like going to McDonalds doesn't make you a Big Mac. You've got to have a personal relationship with Jesus!" And I get that to a degree. It's a call to respond individually and not try to connect with God based on the merits of our family or friends. We don't become Christians as a group but by personally responding to God's message of grace. Yes, Jesus died for the whole world, but any one person is saved

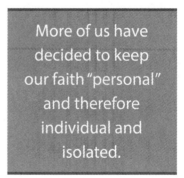

More of us have decided to keep our faith "personal" and therefore individual and isolated.

when he or she individually understands the personal and individual effectiveness of Jesus' death and resurrection, and receives His grace.

However, an unintentional outcome of the church's emphasis on a personal relationship is that more of us have decided to keep our faith "personal" and therefore individual and isolated. We find it uncomfortable to talk about our faith with others, even those within the church. We have difficulty sharing struggles, weaknesses, and sin and, like good Americans, we try to accomplish our Christian life on our own. In fact, one of the reasons you may be reading this book is that you've tried to pull this off on your own and it's not working. Here's the good news: Your journey of faith was never meant to depend solely on you. Rugged individualism may be an iconic American virtue, but it NOT a Christian virtue. From the instant you became a believer, a follower of Jesus, you were automatically enrolled in this thing called the Church, and by it you are instantly and eternally connected with every other believer in Jesus across the world and throughout time. And that's true even if you don't attend a particular church.

But I think the majority of us are missing a proper understanding of what church, or "biblical community," is intended to be. A community of biblical faith plays an essential role in our growth toward God's purpose: it is the vehicle God designed to accomplish our spiritual growth

The word *church* has many meanings. It's the building we go to for an hour or so a week. It's the event that happens on Sunday that typically includes music and a sermon. It's a central organization or denomination. It's an incorporated non-profit. It's a group of people with a common faith. There is some value in each of these definitions, but they all fall short of the Bible's description of church: a community of people united by their shared faith in Jesus as Lord, who are learning, growing, and practicing the Bible together and engaging in the outside world. A biblically functioning church is a group of people who are mutually invested in one another. Even those of us who attend small groups at our churches can miss out on community if the group functions more like a seminar, with each student connected to the teacher but not to each other. The church expresses the truth that we do not need only to be taught, we also need each other! We must be *mutually invested in each other's spiritual growth.*

I believe that many of us are missing God's intention for true biblical community. And there are many reasons for that. In our busy culture, finding time for sincere interaction is tough. Some of our churches have grown quite large, and it's easy to get lost or deliberately hide in them so that few people get to know us. A significant number of churchgoers see no need to get involved beyond an hour-long service. And, while this is rapidly changing, there are still pockets of American culture where people are just assumed to be Christians. They wear their Christian identity as a badge like Republican or Democrat, hunter, fisherman, or Minnesota Vikings fan, but they have no desire to attend church more than a few times a year, if that. The "CEO Christian" (Christmas Easter Only) is a real phenomenon. But is the CEO Christian really a Christian? Even if he is, is he benefiting from the spiritual growth potential residing in the church?

Whatever your church perspective or background, I'd like to take us to the New Testament to better understand a thing or two about the kind of community God intends as the prime environment for our growth and others' redemption. This topic could easily be a book or entire series, so we'll just scratch the surface enough to point us in the right direction.

CREATED, NOT FOUND

Our tendency is to move from place to place searching for the perfect church or Bible study. Even if such a place existed, it would cease to be perfect once we'd joined it! Our mindset should not be to find community, but to create it. I'm not talking about becoming a small group leader or starting your own church. Creating community

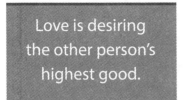

Love is desiring the other person's highest good.

means becoming people who demonstrate love and authenticity and drawing together with others who desire the same. You can do that as a leader, but you can also do that as a follower, with the people you are surrounded by. Small groups in a church are great, but not every small group is truly a biblical community. (Before you go on a tirade against your group or church, my intention is to help us create the kinds of environments that will propel us forward, not criticize what's already in motion.)

The kind of people we are and the motivations we have are critical pieces in creating community. Jesus had a way of loving all people, looking for the outcasts, and including everyone. It was His demeanor and genuine "other-centeredness" that created community wherever He went. No matter who you were or what you'd done, you were welcome with Jesus. Jesus lived without pretense and demonstrated genuine love.

Biblical community is sustained by biblical love. There is a lot of confusion about this word *love*. Countless songs show complete ignorance of the concept. And then it's used in tennis as the term for "zero," which is a reason not to date a tennis player! So what is biblical love? There are a number of good definitions out there, but my favorite is one I learned while studying for my Master's degree in counseling and discipleship: *Love is desiring the other person's highest good.* Love is not about me; it's about you. It's knowing you well enough in light of God's design that I work to make my words and actions promote the highest good in your life. This doesn't always mean you will like what I say and do. It doesn't mean I won't stand up to you or that I'll roll over and always give you your way. If I allow you to take advantage of me without drawing boundaries, I'm not demonstrating biblical love. But when I do draw boundaries, it's because I sincerely desire God's best for you.

1 Corinthians 13 offers a number of great descriptors for love: patient, kind, humble, believing, hoping, and enduring. And the life of Jesus is an amazing model of love in action. Love is both a posture and a movement toward other people. Now you may be thinking, "If I'm all about other people, what about me?" I understand your concern. Many of us have been taken advantage of in the past, and self-protection is a natural response. But biblical love gives us room to care for others while expressing our own desires and sharing our own hearts, trusting God with the outcome. Loving someone means allowing them to love us back.

In addition to love, biblical community requires authenticity. I've sat in small groups where it seemed that people were trying to outdo one another with shows of knowledge or morality or restricting their talk to surface things while hiding serious struggles and problems. I get that being authentic calls for a safe place, but I spent too long searching for such a place and finally decided I need to be involved in creating safety. Many small group guides urge people to share their hearts, without ever teaching the hearers to listen and respond with love, compassion, and humility instead of ranking and judgment. To help create community, I need to be a trustworthy person who is willing to become vulnerable first. I've discovered that others around me long to be authentic too, but they need someone who's willing to go there first. Authenticity requires both time and effort. We become more vulnerable as we grow together, but we must decide from the beginning that we won't settle for surface interactions or outward appearances. We want community, and that requires personal authenticity!

In 2 Timothy 2, Paul exhorts his young protégé to "flee youthful passions and pursue righteousness, faith, love, and peace...." That's the life I want to live. I want be righteous, exhibit faith, learn to truly love, and promote peace. But how do I get there? The answer is in the next phrase: "...along with those who call on the Lord from a pure heart." I love that! "Along with those" says that a life of faith is not a solo sport and not something we can pull off or even express on our own.

I realize that not everyone who attends church or even a small group is looking for anything more than social interaction. And that's too bad, because when you surround yourself with others who truly want to grow in faith and become the people God made us to be, you have the beginning of something special, with everyone growing towards godliness!

> Communication is critical in creating the kind of environment that promotes spiritual growth.

Being authentic requires an atmosphere of grace. Tim Chester puts it this way in his book *How to Change*: "We can be communities of repentance only if we're communities of grace. And this means being honest, open, and transparent about our struggles. We see one another as we really are and accept one another just as Christ accepted us." If we want to create the kind of communities that touch us deeply, grow us forward, and impact others, we need to live in constant awareness of the amazing grace that saves and sustains us. And we must extend that grace to each other. We must know our own shortcomings and imperfections so that we don't expect from others something we can't live up to ourselves! Feeling "safe," as we say we desire, will not happen if we don't extend grace and safety to other people.

COMMUNICATION BUILDS COMMUNITY

Another key element of biblical community is healthy communication. This is what builds authenticity. Again, this subject could easily fill a whole book. Communication is critical in creating the kind of environment that promotes spiritual growth. In my work as a pastor, leader, counselor, and even as a husband and dad, I can confidently say that communication is often what separates the bad from the good and the good from the best when it comes to relationships. We routinely make assumptions about what others think and intend, often without even knowing it. And many of these assumptions are wrong. While much more could be said on this subject, here are five suggestions for improving communication to build community.

1. Communicate what's really going on.

When I say communication promotes growth, I mean the kind of communication that gets below the surface. This requires us to be tuned in and self-aware. When I'm frustrated with a staff member or one of my kids, I need to pause and reflect on why I'm frustrated or I will end up communicating something that is not true or helpful. Before communication can improve anything, I need to understand what is important to me and what is important for the other person to know.

In marriage counseling I've worked with couples who never learned to be in tune with the "why" behind their own thoughts and actions and were therefore unable to communicate authentically with each other. When they learned to reflect on why something bothered them, they could offer insights that might actually improve the interactions. I've also seen this with friends who spent time together but never talked about how the other person impacted them. Here's the reality: If we never have someone who loves us enough to tell us how we impact others, behaviors that could have been corrected end up pushing others away and we're left wondering what we've done wrong. Honest communication is critical for all of us.

2. Communicate to cast vision.

A clear vision for a church, organization, family, or relationship will motivate others and create direction. If we have no idea where we want to be, then we won't know when we get there or how to make good decisions in the right direction. In my experience, people may have a vision (a picture of what their life or relationships could look like) but they rarely take the time to articulate it to themselves or communicate it with others. This leaves people guessing and often results in competing decisions and ongoing frustration. A clear vision is compelling and provides the necessary fuel to push through challenging circumstances. Communicating vision can unite very different people to work hard together, whether in a group of friends, a family, a company, or a church.

3. Communicate to show care.

While love and care are definitely experienced through actions, words also communicate care. In my time as a young leader, it was the people who said "I believe in you" that made all the difference in my perseverance and how I led. There are actually many times as a pastor that I come back to saved emails and short notes or pull something out from my "Encouragement" folder. (Yes, I actually have a folder of notes and cards that people have sent me over the years. I keep them on hand to read when I'm discouraged or don't think I'm making a difference.) Our communication can truly demonstrate we care. Unfortunately, I've met several church staff members who never knew where they stood with their pastors or direct supervisors. How many marriages or families would be radically improved if members communicated their care for one another? Positive words from others really can change an entire atmosphere. I'm not talking about making something up or manipulating by giving false praise. I'm encouraging us to consider what we appreciate about the people in our lives and make the effort to let them know. By doing so, we'll build them up and grow the relationship, and the community.

4. Communicate the tough stuff.

Most of us suffer from an extreme phobia of conflict. (On the other hand, if you enjoy conflict, that's a whole other issue that should be addressed separately.) But if we never wade into the waters of difficult conversation, the best we can hope for is a shallow relationship. I certainly don't enjoy conflict and I dread confrontation, but experience has shown me how much better things can be on the other side. I've worked myself into a state of anxiety and acted awkwardly around others because I was afraid to share my heart and confront someone in my circle. While confrontation is hard, our relationships hold the greatest promise for growth when we're willing to engage in hard conversations—with love and humility, of course.

I'd highly recommend reviewing item #1 in this section before even considering confrontation. We want to make sure we're confronting with truth and not just emotion. We'll go into more detail on this subject in Chapter 7, when we discuss making a difference in the lives of others.

5. Communicate intentionally.

Constructive communication doesn't just happen. We must intentionally take time—or I should say *make* time—to communicate. My wife and I make time for morning coffee before work three or four times a week. We started this a few years ago, and it's reaped valuable results for us. Setting aside these few minutes regularly has strengthened our ability to communicate, decreased opportunities for bad assumptions, and helped us feel more connected.

Don't assume that you know what people are thinking, or that they know what you're thinking. Make the time to communicate. Our weekly church staff meetings and bi-monthly elder meetings, along with countless emails and texts among us, have given our leadership team greater unity and helped us move in the same direction. I know many folks don't enjoy meetings and believe they take time away from more important tasks, but we're finding that our meetings make our work more fruitful. We're doing fewer tasks that don't move the ball down the field toward accomplishing our vision. Good communication promotes our vision and helps us realize our personal, relational, and corporate goals more efficiently and effectively than ever before.

FELLOW JOURNEYERS

When it comes to embracing the something more that God has for us, we must be intentionally speaking life into others and receiving life from them. We have to get to know others, which happens through asking good questions, seeking to understand their motivations, and taking a genuine interest in them. And we have to let others into our lives so they can get us thinking and encourage us as well. Hebrews 10:24-25a states, "And let us consider how to stir up one another to love and good works, not neglecting to meet together, as is the habit of some, but encouraging one another…." In order to consider what will stir up others, I need to know them and think deeply about what will be effective in their lives. Reflecting on these verses keeps us focused on the reason God wants us involved in others' lives: to help us grow in love and service. This growth won't happen unless we're meeting together.

Biblical community is about so much more than socializing. As I write this chapter, I'm sitting in the lobby of a community building at the retirement center where my in-laws live. Moments ago, several folks entered a room to play bingo. As they waited to enter, several older guys sat in sofas around me. They caught up on the events of the past few weeks, complained about other residents, and ribbed one another about their

> Stir one another to become the people God intends us to be.

favorite sports teams. We are social people, and we need one another regardless of our age. But as Christians, we are called to something much deeper and more meaningful than simply socializing or being around others. If our Christian fellowship is limited to conversations about other people, sports, or the weather, we are settling for much less than God intended. No wonder we find ourselves longing for something more.

Biblical community is about gathering a few fellow journeyers, ideally from multiple generations, and doing life together. It's about intentionally engaging in conversations that delve beneath the surface, not to air our dirty laundry but to stir one another to become the people God intends us to be. It's about extending grace to one another as God has extended grace to us. It's about asking good questions and listening for the answers. It's about being committed to one another and desiring the very best for the glory and honor of God.

Having examined the kind of community God intends for us, I wonder how many of us question whether we really need this in our lives. Maybe it's just a guy thing, but most men I know put up a front that we don't need community. We think it's weak to need other people. I've found this to be true even in my role as a husband because I want to prove to my wife that she married well. A few years ago we had a garage sale to throw out—I mean sell—our old stuff. My wife woke me early on Saturday morning to move some stuff to the driveway for the big sale. One of the items on my list was a stackable shelving unit from our laundry room on the lower level. Because I had just got out of bed, I wasn't wearing more than shorts and a t-shirt. I went down to the laundry room and assessed the situation. The unit contained eight shelves connected by wood dowels to form a full bookshelf. I should have asked for help, but I'm a man—the strong, strapping husband my wife trusted with this assignment. So I lifted all eight shelves, holding them together with my wingspan. I got about four feet before the unit came apart from the middle and the shelves tumbled in a pile on top of my bare foot. I screamed cries of praise to Jesus. (Not really, but there were a few religious words in there.) My foot immediately began to puff up and the nail of my big toe was all different shades of purple. For several weeks, my injured foot served as a reminder that I can't do it alone. It's not manlier or more American to do it yourself. In God's economy, independence does not equal freedom. In fact, if we try to do it on our own, we will find ourselves imprisoned by our own stubbornness, setting ourselves up for a downfall.

I can't overemphasize how critical community is. For most of my life, I've been a bit of a loner, an introvert who didn't see a need for deeper relationships. I spent many years as a follower of Jesus trying to live my faith by myself. Sure, I was in small groups and had a number of Christian friends, but I projected what I thought others wanted to see and avoided conversations that went beneath the surface. This got worse when I became a pastor, as I described in the introduction to this book.

My desire to protect my image as a pastor meant that I couldn't let anyone into my life. If they knew the real me—the struggles, the doubts, the frustrations—what would they think? I was left to figure it out on my own, and that didn't go well. I still experienced some spiritual growth, but not in the areas I needed most. I felt more distant and lonely and even began to disconnect from my own thoughts and lose touch with who I was. I began to rationalize my behavior and withhold love from others. I said things like, "Community is for other people, if you're into that kind of thing." This surfacey and self-protective view of community contributed to the collapse of a ministry and an identity.

Your story and your situation may not be as dire as mine was. I'm sure you have lots of good reasons for avoiding the kind of community we've discussed in this chapter. But if I may push a little harder: Don't do it. Don't run from the very environment God has ordained for your growth. It's not easy, it's not convenient, and it's not going to happen unless you go first. But it's what you need, and you will not find something more without it.

After my struggle of 20 years ago, I refuse to live without biblical community. Unfortunately, I haven't often found it in our small group structures (although I do believe it is very possible to create it there). I've had to intentionally arrange conversations with men I've respected, asking to build community together. I've invited people into my life to speak into my story. I've sought biblical counseling at many junctures in my life. I've chosen to live with a greater level of vulnerability, accepting that I may be (and have been) burned by others. But I wouldn't trade any of this for a shallow, socializing connection any day. Biblical community is worth the investment. Not only will you be radically changed because of it, growing towards a fuller image of Jesus Christ, but others will be transformed as well.

SUMMING IT UP

1. Biblical community is created, not found. It requires love and authenticity in an atmosphere of grace.

2. Communication is essential to biblical community. Healthy communication is honest, visionary, caring, willing to address conflict, and intentional.

3. Biblical community is more than just socializing. It's admitting that we need one another as fellow journeyers in faith.

CHAPTER 6

MORE ENGAGEMENT:
Maximize Your Potential

I've always been a big believer in potential. When I worked with students as a youth pastor, I tended to believe in the kids whom others wrote off, because I saw the potential of what they could become. I gave kids opportunities on mission trips or during weekly programs to develop their gifts and to demonstrate that they were more than what others thought they were—or worse, told them they were. Every summer, I renew my hope in my Brooklyn Nets basketball team as I read up on the rookies and watch videos of the free agents signed because I see the potential of what could be. You could call me a fan who doesn't accept reality, but I like to think of myself as someone who finds hope in *potential* reality. Hope is what drives us forward, after all. Hope is critical to life! (Hebrews 11:1)

When I first walked into Grace Church, where I serve as the lead pastor, I saw potential. Sure there were things that concerned me, habits and characteristics that were dated and spent, but God gave me eyes to see what our church could become. Since that day in 2006, Grace Church has become something very special, the healthiest church I've ever been part of. I am humbled to know that we got to where we are because many people believed in God for big things and worked to make them reality. And the exciting thing is, we still have room for growth.

I could introduce you to many friends, former students, staff members, and teammates who allowed me the privilege of speaking into their lives and calling out unrealized potential. And they have done the same for me. With a vision of what could be, we have surpassed our own expectations.

Here's what I know about you: God created you with incredible potential. You have something really special to give the world and the Kingdom He is building. As you learn to identify and express it, you will experience personal joy and others will benefit from your contribution. I hope people in your life have called this out in you, but if not, allow me. I don't have to know you personally to know that you are special and that God has more awaiting you than what you know today.

For any number of reasons, many of us underestimate ourselves and miss out on what could be. One of the reasons I wrote this book is that I believe in your potential, and I want something more for you and the people you will influence.

POWERFUL WORDS

I wouldn't be in ministry today if it weren't for someone, or rather many someones, who chose to believe in me. People saw something in me that I didn't see in myself. They spoke words of life to me and gave me tangible opportunities to experiment with different gifts. They taught me to view every person and situation I encounter with eyes that see beyond the present reality to what could be. And while we all know that words can be incredibly encouraging, there are others who use words to tear down.

As a high school freshman, I played on the basketball team. My body was growing faster than my coordination, and a pass thrown at high velocity was an incredible challenge for me to catch. The guys on my team thought it would be brilliant to combine my last name with my lack of coordination, and so my nickname became "Stonehands." That was one of many instances during high school that led to a low self-image and caused me to be one of the quieter guys in school, keeping to my two friends and trying not to make waves. But I was fortunate that my whole life was not wrapped up in that public high school. I had a church life that was quite the opposite from my experience in high school.

Just before high school, I was serving as a counselor at a day camp my church hosted every summer. There was an opening on the staff for a third grade Bible teacher. This involved preparing a 45-minute Bible class for 30 to 40 squirming grade-school students every morning for six weeks. It was a position typically reserved for adults, often teachers who had the summers off. Sara, the camp director, saw something in me and decided to believe in my potential. She gave me the job and set me on a path of significant growth. While I'm not sure how much those kids remembered, they saw my passion and love and it had an impact on them and on me. I gained confidence and had the chance to grow as a communicator.

Likewise, a youth pastor named Virgil saw leadership abilities in me and gave me opportunities to serve on the student leadership team. In fact, right before he left to pursue God's call at another church he put me in a key leadership role in the middle school program. As a high school senior, I had the chance to lead others and watch our youth group more than double in size in the six months I was in leadership! In these environments, I had the chance to experiment, try, fail, learn, and hone the abilities God gave me.

> God created you in His image and gifted you for a purpose.

After high school, I attended Bible college in preparation for a career in ministry. Before that point, I was focused on a business degree due to modest success in the business program at my high school. However, through weekly trips to a park near my home for prayer and reflection, I came to understand that God had a different path for me. God showed me that some of my leadership and organizational abilities could be used in ministry work.

After my freshman year in college, I worked part-time as the youth director of a small church in New Jersey. It was there that I met Casey, a man in his eighties who loved Jesus and loved the church. We immediately became friends. When I was around him, I felt much more important than I actually was. Casey had a gift for making people feel special, and for some reason he believed in me. His support made me want to be better, to grow into the person he believed I could be. Near the end of his life, there was a celebration for him and his legacy. At his invitation, I drove 90 minutes from my college to join the hundreds of people who attended this special event in his honor. I couldn't believe it when the emcee of the event made special note of my presence during the celebration service. Here were all these bigwigs attending, and Casey had made sure I felt special.

I stand on the shoulders of some amazing people. The point in telling you about just a few of these people is to illustrate the power of believing in someone's potential. I don't know your story. I don't know how long you've been a follower of Jesus, nor if you've had a Sara, Virgil, or Casey in your life. But I do know this about you: God created you in His image and gifted you for a purpose. If you're a believer, His Holy Spirit lives in you. You have amazing potential to make an impact in this world and for His Kingdom. Not only will others' lives be changed, but you will experience more and more of the life God made you to experience!

In Ephesians 4:13, Paul writes about remaining faithful "until we all reach unity in the faith and in the knowledge of the Son of God and become mature, attaining to the whole measure of the fullness of Christ" (NIV). Consider this in light of our discussion of something more. Every Christian should long for this type of maturity—a maturity that brings us the whole measure of the fullness of Christ. This is what Paul desired for himself and had not yet attained, according to Philippians 3. This drive for something more is what keeps us focused on the true purpose for our lives. We don't make the most of our gifts and get active in our faith because it's our duty, but because it's what we long for. When we attain to the whole measure of the fullness of Christ, we align ourselves with Jesus, who is the head of the body. So the body is aligned with the head. The "fullness of Christ" is achieved when our thoughts are the thoughts of God. It's embracing God's original intention.

But let's look closer at the verses leading up to Ephesians 4:13. It's in the preceding verses that we discover *how* fullness and maturity are actualized. Let's look at verse 11: "So Christ himself gave the apostles, the prophets, the evangelists, the pastors and teachers...." Jesus gives us various people with various gifts of leadership for a distinct purpose in the church. And that purpose is seen in the next verse: "...to **equip his people** for works of service...." So good, godly leaders put something into and bring something out of the people in their faith community.

Obviously, the people themselves have a part to play here as well. Let's keep reading in verse 12-13: "...so that the body of Christ may be built up until we all reach unity in the faith and in the knowledge of the Son of God and become mature, attaining to the whole measure of the fullness of Christ." The knowledge Paul is talking about here is an experiential knowledge, a knowledge that can't be developed from reading and study alone. It's a relational, interactive knowledge that can only be fostered through time and participation in a personal friendship with Jesus and with His people. There is something about a healthy church and Christians working together that produces the life and experience we all long for deep down.

In Romans 12:6, Paul says it this way: "We have different gifts, according to the grace given to each of us" (NIV). And Peter writes in 1 Peter 4:10: "Each of you should use whatever gift you have received to serve others, as faithful stewards of God's grace in its various forms" (NIV). My guess is that if you've been around church at all you've heard these verses used to talk about the need for more nursery workers or parking lot attendants. Maybe you've even felt guilty as you heard these verses. But I'd like to reframe this for you. Our spiritual gifts and natural talents are among the primary tools

> All people have worth and dignity because they bear God's image.

God has given each of us so that we can live the life He created us to live. They are not primarily about filling programmatic gaps in the church, but about attaining maturity and fullness in Christ, while adding true spiritual value to God's Kingdom. Yes, the church grows when we all do this, but don't overlook the benefit in your personal spiritual growth. If we believe that we can attain something more without active investment of our time and abilities, we are naive to God's design.

THE PURPOSE FOR OUR POTENTIAL

When it comes to discovering and developing our spiritual gifts, I think we often jump into the *how* without taking time to understand the *why*. And then we wonder why our motivation fizzles out. Understanding our gifts, and how to use them appropriately, thereby maximizing of our spiritual potential, all require effort. We need to stay fueled up and oriented by understanding the purpose for

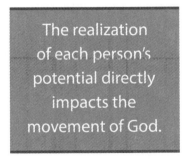

The realization of each person's potential directly impacts the movement of God.

our potential. And to understand our purpose, we need to know a few things about our identity.

First, **all humanity is created in the image of God**. That means God designed us with some of the same stuff found in Himself. This should shape how we view ourselves, and others too. All people have worth and dignity because they bear God's image. Now we don't have a lot of time to get into the theology, but we know that God's image in us has been marred by sin. So now all human beings have both dignity (because of God's image) and depravity (because of sin). We don't want to emphasize one of those aspects without recognizing its opposite, but for the purpose of this chapter, I want you to see the amazing potential and dignity within you because you were created in God's image! As Aslan says to King Peter in C. S. Lewis's *Chronicles of Narnia,* "You come of the Lord Adam and the Lady Eve. And that is both honor enough to erect the head of the poorest beggar, and shame enough to bow the shoulders of the mightiest emperor in earth."

Second, **all Christians have the Holy Spirit alive and active in them**. If you've come to the point where you've transferred your faith and trust to Jesus, then the Bible is clear that the Holy Spirit lives in you. Think about that for a second. The same Spirit that raised Jesus from the dead is alive in you! The same Spirit that produces things like love, joy, peace, patience, kindness, and self-control is at work in every believer.

I was raised in a church that tended to downplay the role of the Holy Spirit. I think this came from skepticism toward what was called the "charismatic movement." I understand that there has been abuse of teachings of the Spirit in some churches, but the downplaying of the Spirit's real role caused me to depend on myself and my own efforts to create growth. As I now understand, the Spirit frees me from self-reliance and creates greater dependence on God because it's actually His Spirit who does the work. The Spirit makes it happen, and I merely cooperate or partner with God's work. As a Christian, you have an incredible, supernatural potential because of the Spirit's work in and through you!

Recognizing that our gifts are given by the Spirit reminds us that they serve a greater purpose than our own fulfillment. In the book of Acts—which could have been named the "Acts of the Spirit"—we see a demonstration of the Spirit in a small band of Jesus-followers who form community to impact the world. There is a purpose behind the uniqueness of each person. The realization of each person's potential directly impacts the movement of God. I want us to realize the magnitude of our potential due to the Spirit's involvement. Now think about this: If even half of the Christians who attend churches are not living up to their spiritual potential, imagine the impact on the movement of the Spirit in our world—not to mention the impact on the individuals sitting in church and missing out on God's design for something more.

Third in our discussion of identity, **all Christians are given at least one spiritual gift**. As we saw earlier, Paul and Peter both affirm that God has graciously given each of us supernatural gifts for the fulfillment of His mission in the world, for the building up of His church, and for our personal growth, maturity, and fullness. There are gifts like speaking, leadership, hospitality, mercy, service, and many others. (See Romans 12, 1 Corinthians 12, and 1 Peter 4 for a more complete list). Regardless of what you were told growing up or what you tend to think about yourself, you have Spirit-powered potential to grow personally and to impact the lives of countless others for the glory of God! How's that for a self-image boost?

You will never really know what it means to be a Christian until you allow God to use you and your gifts for His mission and purpose. I've met too many people in churches who either underestimate the importance of getting involved or who become involved merely to satisfy their own guilt or a perceived need within the church. I hope you're seeing how maximizing your God-given potential is a key step in experiencing something more. For some of us, this may be the one step that brings immediate growth and passion to our faith. But *how* you approach this step makes all the difference.

MAXIMIZE YOUR POTENTIAL

So how do you discover and develop your spiritual gifts in order to maximize their effectiveness? Here are some suggestions.

1. Pay attention to your story and isolate the trends and commonalities.

I often lead people through an exercise: Choose six pivotal events from your life. Three events should be positive, meaning they shaped and likely encouraged you. Three events should be negative or painful, and have also shaped you: for example, a betrayal may have made you less likely to trust. Now plot the three highs and three lows on a timeline beginning with age three or four on the left and ending with your current age on the right. While your life includes many more than six significant events, you'll likely discover some trends by reflecting on the events you've plotted. In the first place, there's a reason you identified each event as negative or positive. Your choices reflect your values and your approach to life. The events you chose indicate what you're passionate about.

Another approach is to make a long list of things—events, experiences, adventures—you've enjoyed from a young age until today and then ask yourself, "What did I like about this activity?" Grab a pad or journal and write down what you discover. As you do, you will likely discover some commonalities that provide insight into how you're wired and what brings satisfaction to your life. Whether you choose to do one or both of these exercises, the key is to reflect on the events you've identified. Look for patterns, similar things that excite you or are important to you. Pay attention to the values that come out in your reaction to these events. Look closely at your role in the event; what were *you* doing and how did it make you feel alive? Write out your reflections without pushing for a conclusion. Simply notice what's there, and you'll discover truths rising to the surface. These exercises will move you toward finding your God-given role in His Kingdom, which is a key indicator of giftedness.

2. Utilize multiple assessments.

There are a number of different tests and assessments designed to help us understand ourselves. If you Google "spiritual gifts test," you'll find a combination of free and paid services that will provide some insight. There are also a number of books available that will take you even deeper as they guide you through the process of self-discovery. I've even participated in assessments performed by a trained coach. These are probably the most effective, but also the most expensive. For most of us, a free or low-cost assessment is more than sufficient, especially when combined with the other tools in this chapter.

I caution you against putting too much stock in any one tool. I've seen people take a twenty-question assessment and assume that what it told them was gospel truth. Any assessment is helpful, but it should not preclude us from experimenting in activities outside of an identified "sweet spot." This leads us to our next tool.

3. Experiment.

Spiritual gifts are given to benefit the whole body of Christ, both the local faith community and the worldwide Kingdom of God. We should all explore and experiment with different areas and opportunities to serve God and others. Be slow to specialize. As you find things that draw forth both enjoyment and effectiveness, ask yourself why. Sometimes you may love a particular ministry because of the people you serve with or the health of the ministry itself and not because it's truly your sweet spot. When you've truly discovered a spiritual gift, you will likely experience joy and impact regardless of who you serve with or the nature of the ministry. You can then begin to specialize by serving in areas that utilize your gifts in your preferred environment.

4. Do it in and for community.

In Ephesians 4 and other texts that discuss spiritual gifts and ministry involvement, the intention is clearly to use our gifts as part of a team and for the benefit of all. None of us has all the gifts. We need each other! We must value others and their gifts as critically important to the overall goal. When we serve as a team, the whole team wins and God gets the glory. Our reason for serving is to help the whole community grow and be transformed. We do it for others. Sure, we'll come alive as individuals, but our motivation should be to bless others.

5. Get feedback.

I've had the awkward experience of talking with a few people who thought they had certain gifts that they clearly didn't have. That's not to say skills can't be developed, but gifts come supernaturally and provide a solid foundation for further growth. It's hard to see someone lose confidence due to misidentifying a supposed area of giftedness. But if we remain humble and teachable, asking feedback from those who see us in action, we'll gain great insight. I'm not suggesting you let others' opinions alone steer you. Pay attention to what you enjoy and what brings you life. But God places us in community for a purpose, and He will use others to assist you in identifying and developing your gifts. Sometimes that means others will call out the gifts we take for granted. I remember commenting on a particular worship leader's ability to set an audience at ease. He had assumed everyone knew how to do this. I assured him this is not the case. He has a unique gift. Until someone pointed it out to him, he'd never considered developing and expanding this gift.

Experiencing something more is not a passive venture.

Spiritual gifts aren't given to us in a fully mature form. They can and should be deliberately cultivated. What was significant about the opportunities I received as a young ministry leader was that they came with coaching, encouragement, and a team of others. Our gifts must be refined and implemented as part of a community of faith.

6. Do for others what you wish had been done for you.

Maybe you've been blessed with a spiritual mentor who called out your gifts and helped you refine them. You are fortunate!

Our spiritual gifts and passions are secret weapons in the fight against darkness and stagnation. We need places where we can believe in one another. We need sincere encouragement from others. That's not to say we should pump people up without purpose or substance, or in areas where they're not gifted. But let's notice when others are serving in their sweet spot. Let's speak life and encouragement to them. When we build this kind of culture around us, we'll find that we benefit as well.

Experiencing something more is not a passive venture. There is potential inside each of us, a potential placed there by God. Beyond your spiritual gifts, your background and experiences give you a unique perspective that can help others. There are certain people you'll impact more significantly than others. While there are likely a few reasons for this, one will be the experiences you have in common. God wants to redeem your painful past events by using what you've learned to benefit others. And the specific individuals who have shaped and influenced you have prepared you for great impact in certain environments.

Remember the biblical account of Esther? She was placed in a position of royalty as the queen. When her people were in danger, she had a voice with the king to make a positive difference. What an amazing example of how God places people just like you and me in places where our background and abilities can make a real impact. Just like Esther, you are uniquely prepared to forward the mission of God in the lives of others. Get involved, learn all you can about how God has made you, and then practice your gifts and skills inside of biblical community.

SUMMING IT UP

1. God has given each Jesus-follower spiritual gifts to bring us to maturity within the context of a healthy church. Spiritual gifts allow us to grow personally while also serving the church and God's Kingdom.

2. As Christians, the purpose of our potential is a reflection of our identity: made in God's image, indwelt by God's Spirit, and entrusted with at least one spiritual gift.

3. Discovering and developing your spiritual gifts involves paying attention to your story, using assessment tools, experimenting, serving in community, seeking feedback, and investing in others.

CHAPTER 7

MORE COURAGE:
Make a Difference

I am amazed at the number of movies and television shows about superheroes. As I write this book, there are superhero shows on television every night of the week. In the summer, blockbuster movies feature heroes of all shapes and sizes. When I was growing up, superheroes were for kids. No longer! Today, I see more adults at Marvel and DC hero movies than I do kids—and I'm kind of glad, because some of the content is not real "kid friendly."

What is our fascination with superheroes? Why are we willing to spend many hours and a lot of dollars immersing ourselves in hero stories? I wonder if it has something to do with our world. We live in a dark place that seems to be getting darker. Life on earth is complex and often seems hopeless, as if only someone with super powers could change our landscape. And maybe our fascination reflects an inner desire. Do we secretly long to be more courageous? Do we wish we could make a difference, but instead just live vicariously through our superheroes? Isn't it interesting that many of these heroes began life as everyday, ordinary, maybe even overlooked kinds of people?

The longing to be a hero seems to be hardwired into us. My heart beats faster when I watch a movie where the guy sweeps in and beats the bad guy and saves the girl. I wish I could be that courageous. But courage doesn't require wearing a mask and stopping criminals. How about caring enough about another person to call them on their sin? How about taking a risk and investing in another's life to be a positive influence?

THE CALL FOR COURAGE

Our world needs courageous people. Sadly, in our fast-paced culture we've become ever more connected, but simultaneously more isolated. The evil one (Satan) has succeeded in convincing us to do life on our own. We're afraid to speak into one another's lives for fear of rejection or belief that it's not our place. Growth has been reduced to self-help books and inspiring seminars, where we can remain anonymous and therefore isolated. The practice of mentoring and shaping one another up close and personal is increasingly rare. Because we are more alone, we've begun to care more and more about ourselves and believe a lie that others don't really need us.

More than once, my wife has told me about a conversation with someone followed by a description of what she really wanted to say. I've sometimes asked, knowing full well that she held her tongue, "What did they say when you told them that?" I know that Lisa has some amazing insights and could offer some great counsel, but her own fears of whether people would be receptive to

> Courage is moving forward because you believe that something is more important than your fear.

this often keep her from sharing truth in love. My wife is one of the most courageous people I know. Yet even she fears hurting someone's feelings or feels that it's not her place to speak.

But our world needs us, our churches need us, and other Christians need us to step forward with courage. Growth happens in and around us when we step out of our comfort zones and into the scary unknown. I think one of the reasons we fail to experience something more is that we've prioritized living safe. We've rested in our comfort zones. Think about this: you won't feel that your faith has meaning and purpose if you're not truly living by faith. Growth happens and life is truly lived when we step into the "danger zone." The comfort zone is where we go to wait until we die. I'm overstating to make a point, but I hope you see that living the lives we were meant to live requires courage.

Many of us believe that truly courageous people are not afraid. But courage is not a lack of fear; rather, courage is doing right in spite of fear. Courage and fearlessness are not synonyms. Courage is

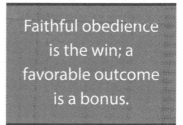

Faithful obedience is the win; a favorable outcome is a bonus.

moving forward because you believe that something is more important than your fear. If you're afraid of what someone will think of you, then your love for them and desire for their best must become stronger than your fear. If you're afraid of the social consequence of living your faith, then your love for God and desire for His blessing must grow stronger than your fear. Think about what you're afraid to do and what would need to grow stronger in order for you to exercise courage. Courage is choosing to strengthen godly desire until it overcomes the fear that holds you back. Making a difference in the world requires courage, but the God who strengthens us is bigger than any fear we might face.

Consider the story of Shadrach, Meshach, and Abednago, the three guys who get thrown into a furnace in the book of Daniel. I love their comment before they're thrown in: "If this be so, our God whom we serve is able to deliver us from the burning fiery furnace, and he will deliver us out of your hand, O king. *But if not,* be it known to you, O king, that we will not serve your gods or worship the golden image that you have set up" (Daniel 3:17-18, emphasis added). God is able to intervene, these guys are saying, *but even if He doesn't* we won't lose faith. If things don't turn out as we'd like, it's not because God could not have intervened, but He chose in His divine wisdom to allow a different outcome. On the surface this may not feel very reassuring, but I'd rather be in the center of God's will and in His presence than to be separate from Him, doing my own thing for a temporarily favorable outcome. Faithful obedience is the win; a favorable outcome is a bonus (and certainly not an indicator of whether you followed God's will).

For a picture of faithful obedience, let's return to a passage I briefly introduced in Chapter 1, Hebrews 5:12-14: "In fact, though by this time you ought to be teachers, you need someone to teach you the elementary truths of God's word all over again. You need milk, not solid food! Anyone who lives on milk, being still an infant, is not acquainted with the teaching about righteousness. But solid food is for the mature, who by constant use have trained themselves to distinguish good from evil" (NIV).

So what is happening in this passage? In context, it's not likely that the author is addressing new believers. Rather, his message seems to be for believers who have gone backwards, away from what they once were. Some scholars think these believers were attempting to sidestep their responsibility in a world that persecuted them by regressing to a more "infant," less controversial state. It's not that they didn't know what was true and right, but they had stopped practicing and living this way.

This passage also gives us some insight into God's intentions for us as followers of Jesus. First we see that we "ought to be teachers." Obviously we don't all have the spiritual gift of teaching, but the author is pointing out that we all ought to be influencers and guides for others. We need to take initiative to engage in the lives of other people for the purpose of their spiritual enlightenment and progress.

Secondly, his goal is that we are skilled in "the teaching of righteousness." The world needs true followers of the Word who have developed the maturity and skills to live like Jesus. I love the word "skilled" (which is used in the ESV version) because it implies much more than knowledge. It's not just that we *know* the Word but that we're skilled in applying it correctly to the necessary situations.

The only way to become skilled is to take what we've learned and practice it in the real world. I remember when I was first learning to play basketball. I read a few books, watched a few videos, and listened to a few instructors. But the way I became proficient was to ride my bike to the outdoor basketball court at my middle school and spend hours practicing what I had learned. This is when my knowledge became skill. If we don't learn what God says *and then practice living it,* we will remain spiritual infants.

One of the biggest surprises to me as I've grown in my faith is to discover how many people in our churches have been Christians for many years, often practically all their lives, and yet are not skilled in the "word of righteousness." To be honest with you, I've been significantly hurt by the words and actions of so-called "mature" Christians who were clearly still infants in the faith. I hope you'll take this chapter to heart not only for the goal of experiencing the life God intended for you, but also because our churches are in desperate need of many more Christians who are skilled in the word of righteousness and in all the aspects of a mature and balanced life in Jesus Christ.

The last phrase I want to pull out of this passage is "by constant use have trained themselves to distinguish good from evil." Discernment is a critical skill not just for our own benefit but also that we may guide others. Our world is more complex than ever before. Issues that once seemed black and white are now more gray. Often we find ourselves in situations that are not specifically covered in the Bible. This is where discernment is critical. Too often we make decisions and give advice based on emotion, sympathy, or fear of what others will think. Notice what the author tells us: Discernment is a skill to master by training! Over and over again we must practice applying biblical principles to real life situations, regardless of the response from others who may not be operating from the same foundation.

Discernment is required even in our churches, among other Christians. I've made the mistake of assuming that because another Christian did something or said it was okay, I could do it as well. I remember a gathering of Christians at someone's house while I was in college. The hosts put on a movie with some graphic scenes of sexuality. As all of us single young adults were watching, I thought to myself, "This is not right." While I got up and walked into another room, neither I nor anyone else was courageous enough to stand up and say, "This isn't appropriate for us."

We must become proficient in discerning not just good versus bad but good versus best. Once we land on our convictions, we must express and act on them with courage, but also humility and grace toward others who think differently.

COURAGE IN ACTION

All right, so now that you're motivated to trust God and move forward in courage, how do you do it? Let's get practical! Making a difference requires taking a step.

1. Step away from the sidelines.

In junior high, we had dances in the gym on the first Friday night of every month. Even though I wasn't interested in dancing and wasn't one of the cool kids in my middle school, I went. I remember standing by the wall with most of the other guys. Really, junior high dances should have been called "stands" because the vast majority of us stood there rather than dancing. We watched the few classmates who dared to enter the dance floor like we were watching animals at the zoo. I was scared

> We must leave the sidelines if we're going to make an impact in our world.

to death to ask anyone to dance and even more scared that someone would ask me. So I stayed by the wall while the music played. Similarly, when I graduated to high school and played for the freshman basketball team, I distinctly remember hoping no one would throw me the ball because I might mess up and miss a big shot.

These experiences show that sidelines can be immensely attractive. If we never step out, we can never mess up. We tell ourselves it's safer on the sidelines, where we can get credit for being there without having to do anything. We can live vicariously through those who are on the field playing without getting dirty or tired ourselves. That sounds nice, but when you stay on the sidelines you never move forward.

You know what I came to realize? The ordinary guys with a little bit of courage got to dance with the cute girls. The not-so-great athletes who wanted the ball and worked for it got to take the big shots, and make some of them, and so became better athletes. We must leave the sidelines if we're going to make an impact in our world.

While this chapter focuses on making a difference with our gifts and passions, leaving the sidelines can have other practical results in our lives. I've seen so many people at a standstill in a relationship because neither person was willing to leave the sidelines. Neither person was willing to be the first to love, the first to serve, the first to forgive, or the first to ask for forgiveness. Instead of waiting for the other person to do what we think they should do, we should be the first to leave the sidelines and take a risk. This is where life is found—in a place of action, not a place of waiting, spectating, or blaming others.

2. Step out and take a risk.

As we're learning, making a difference will not happen if we play it safe. We must be willing to risk our comfort and step into the game. Engagement will look different for each of us, but my guess is you know when you're on the sidelines and when you're in the game. Our involvement is not a duty but an intentional leap into something more. Our action is a step of faith and growth. We are part of a movement of God, and often this will feel like a risk. What if it doesn't work out the way we hoped it would? What if we don't enjoy it? What if it becomes more energy-draining and less life-giving? Reality checks are important, but "what if" questions can smother the courage of godly obedience.

Some years ago now, I went out to breakfast with some friends from the church I was then serving in. When we had finished eating, we split the bill and I told them I would settle up with the restaurant. As I stood at the cash register after my friends had left, my eyes wandered and I connected with a guy sitting alone in a booth eating his breakfast. I thought nothing of it and began to walk out. All of a sudden I felt a nudge, and my mind started talking to me. "Jason, go back and buy that guy's breakfast!" That's the stupidest thing I've ever heard, I thought to myself. But then I wondered, what if God put that thought there? Again, I questioned myself. "You're being ridiculous. Just because you're a Christian does not mean that every thought in your head is put there by God!" So I kept walking and put the key in my car door and sat in the driver's seat. But the thought came again. "Buy that guy's breakfast!" Okay, I thought, this is absurd. God does not get involved in breakfast! And even if I did go back, what would I say? "Umm, excuse me sir, but God told me to buy your breakfast." And he would say, "Sure he did, pal. Have you taken your meds today?"

Then I had another thought. "What if you're running from God? What if God really is prompting you and you're disobeying Him? What kind of Christian would you be if you didn't go back?" So you know what? I did it. I went back and placed seven bucks on the guy's table and said, "Can I buy your breakfast today?" He looked a little shocked. He asked my name and told me his name was Willie.

And then Willie said, "I overheard you guys talking over there and it sounded like you were involved in some good stuff, helping people and other things." I said, "Yeah, we're involved in a church. And you might think I'm crazy, but I think God told me to buy your breakfast." He replied, "Well, God bless you!" So I told him a little about our church and where we were located. And then would you believe that Willie showed up at our church that weekend? He became a follower of Jesus and ended up telling his whole neighborhood about the guy who'd bought him breakfast and brought him to Jesus, and I think something like 438 more people became Christians as a result, and a mission agency was begun in my name.

Actually none of that last part is true. But isn't that what we think should happen when we step out in faith? God rewards us with major impact, right? The truth is I never saw Willie again after that day. I don't know if he walked away thinking his free breakfast was purchased by a crazy Jesus person or if it really impacted him. But that's not the point, is it? Our obedience is less about the Willies of the world and more about the Jasons—

people like you and me who are willing to step out, take a risk, be a part of God's work, and leave the results up to Him. Again, obedience is the win; a favorable outcome is a bonus!

I don't know what God's next step looks like for you, but I can tell you that it's worth taking. Don't ever minimize or underestimate the power of simple steps of faith in a Godward direction! The thought of talking to that specific person may be really scary. Or the idea of getting involved in that specific ministry may seem incredibly time consuming. The habits and actions suggested in this book may seem like they're for super Christians, not average Joes. But listen, you don't have to do it all. Just do something! Take your next step forward, and after that step take the next one. No need for a huge leap forward or a monumental change. And if your next step *is* something big, or something that feels big to you, talk to God about it. He will lead you and then, yes, you do need to follow.

3. Trust God to guide your steps.

Here's the thing, and I've said this more than once about a life of something more: this is not a self-help movement. It's not a new set of to-do's to add to your crowded list of religious activity. This is about walking with God and doing life with God. It's about seeing Him in real time, experiencing the life He wants to bless you with. In short, this is an act of trust.

For years, I believed that trust was something I did mentally. I thought that if I learned enough information about someone or something, I could trust it. But trust is not merely intellectual, and this is where I think so many Christians get it wrong. We say we're trusting God, but really we're just intellectually agreeing that God is trustworthy. We trust God by stepping out, taking His Word as actual truth—not truth to argue about, not truth just to memorize, but truth to live.

Another flawed understanding of trust is confidence in someone's actions instead of their character. I've heard people say, "I used to trust so and so and then they did this thing I didn't like." This is a dangerous definition of trust; in fact, it may not be trust at all. Granted, there's a difference between trusting people and trusting God. But here's the truth: God will allow things and even do things we may not like, things that scare us or require us to wait. If we abandon God in the process, which so many do, can we really say that we're trusting Him?

I'm not saying that everything God asks us to do makes complete sense. I'm not going to promise that you'll always see the "why" behind God's actions or promptings. But trusting Him means sticking with Him and seeing it through. Trust isn't about God doing things the way you would do them; it's about God's character. God is trustworthy. We trust who He is even when His actions don't line up with what we want. How many people in the Bible didn't see the why or even the eventual outcome until much later, or not at all? Trusting God means following His heart even when I can't see His hands.

Trust is active and positive. Christianity has developed a reputation for being against things. The focus tends to be on what we abstain from, what we avoid, and what we think other people should stop doing. But God is looking for action, not avoidance. Here's how Erwin McManus puts it in his book *Chasing Daylight*: "We have put so much emphasis on avoiding evil that we have become virtually blind to the endless opportunities for doing good. We have defined holiness through what we separate ourselves from rather than what we give ourselves to. I am convinced the great tragedy is not the sins we commit, but the life that we fail to live. You cannot follow God in neutral."

True faith is about looking at God and looking at our circumstances, and being more certain about our God than our circumstances. We move forward and engage in His mission from a place of trust. That is the basis for practically every Old Testament story of triumph. God uses small acts of faith to make a big difference, whether it's the parting of the Red Sea, the crumbling of the walls of Jericho, or the endless oil that poured out for the poor woman and her son.

4. Take a step to catalyze a response.

A catalyst is something that initiates or causes events to happen. As we've discussed, stepping forward in faith can impact others in positive ways. I talk often about the power of a simple invitation to church and the ripple effect it can have on others. I'll confess that I often prefer to talk to and hang out with people I already know. Meeting new folks can be a challenge for me, especially those who are not part of my community. But I'm willing to be challenged when I consider the real impact that a simple gesture or conversation can have in real people's lives.

We induce others toward motion when we are in motion. When we step out in trust and move forward, God uses our faithfulness to convict and motivate others to do the same. As we discussed in an earlier chapter, we are made for community and meant to do life as a team. We can't afford to function as individuals with no concern for others around us. We must take responsibility for other followers of Jesus because when we come together for God's mission, we catalyze a movement.

Have you ever considered that our actions might catalyze a response from God as well? Think about the major movements in our world that began with a step of faith, an intentional act which God took and multiplied in impact. Riding a bus, making a speech, gathering to pray, giving away the last bit of food, and countless other little steps have activated God's power in incredible ways. It's astonishing to think about my actions affecting God in any way, but they do. God delights in moving in and through our acts of trust and steps of faith.

OVERCOMING OBJECTIONS

Before we leave this chapter, I want to address two objections that are sometimes made when it comes to engaging, particularly with those outside of the faith.

1. What if I get involved with others and they assume I'm endorsing their lifestyle?

Sometimes when we engage with people who are far from God, we fear that our love and grace will be interpreted as approval of their sinful behavior. There seems to be a fine line between accepting the person and accepting their behavior. But remember this: proximity doesn't equal permission. Just because we're around sinful activity doesn't mean that we're giving permission for it. Jesus spent a lot of time with sinners and was often accused of being contaminated by sinners, but that couldn't be further from the truth.

It's also worth remembering that before someone is a believer, they haven't signed up for God's values or behavior. Christians aren't called to be the morality police or the referees blowing whistles at people who aren't even in the game. Don't focus on people's behavior; focus on their hearts. When God changes someone's heart, their lifestyle follows. And we are not called to do the Holy Spirit's work in peoples' lives; we're just arranging the meeting. Sometimes I think the fear that we might endorse sinful behavior is an excuse for not getting in the game. Love people well, lead people to Jesus, and let Him take it from there. As my friend Jim Gustafson says, "Our job is to fish, not catch. To bear witness, not convict. To love, not transform."

Another aspect of this question relates to our own distinctiveness and holiness. While few of us would verbalize it this way, there seems to be a fear that we'll "catch" sin from being around sinners as we might catch a virus from someone who's sick. While I agree that placing ourselves in tempting situations has risk, I've found this to be another holy-sounding excuse for not engaging with lost people. Contact doesn't equal contamination. Jesus was able to remain holy in an environment of sinners. And remember, you or I might be the single source of light in an otherwise dark place.

2. What if another Christian doesn't want my involvement in their life?

This is a question worth wrestling through. As a general principle, the closer the relationship, the better the chance for impact. I've found that when another person truly believes you are *for* them, they are much more likely to welcome your involvement. If you've grown up in church, you've likely had multiple experiences with church people you barely knew getting involved where they shouldn't. Again, however well-meaning, it's not our purpose to be the morality police. But if we could learn to develop the kind of relationships and communities I've described in this book, we could influence and impact other Christians from a place of love.

> God wants us to be difference-makers, not passive information-receivers.

I've also found that asking permission is a helpful tactic in coming alongside another person, Christian or not. We can ask permission simply by saying, "I've noticed some things that may be helpful for you. Would you be open to hearing them?" As a husband I've found this skill to be incredibly helpful in conversations with my wife. Like most guys I know, I'm wired to fix things. When my wife shares an issue that's on her heart, I salivate at the chance to jump in and fix it. This has typically not been received well by Lisa. So lately I've been saying, "You know, as you were talking I thought of a few things that may be helpful. But I also realize that it's great just to have someone to listen. Let me know if you're ready for some thoughts or suggestions; otherwise, I'm happy to listen." I know it may sound scripted, but I'm sincere. My desire to fix is based on my love for my wife. I want her to have healthy and happy experiences. Even though it feels good to fix, my love for her is the higher goal. And loving someone might mean asking permission to speak into their life. We might even say, "You mentioned you wanted to grow in a certain area. Would it be helpful if I held you accountable by asking you about it every now and then?"

This may sound like a lot of work, but please don't shy away from it. This is what God intends Christian community to be. We need to love each other and love God's design (people without sin) enough to speak into each other's lives. God wants us to be difference-makers, not passive information-receivers. The Coach is calling you off the bench and into the game. In spite of your fears, discover the courage that God gives freely. Engage with those who don't know Jesus and promote God's best in the lives of fellow believers. Let's do this! Let's get off the sidelines and experience something more.

SUMMING IT UP

1. Growth occurs when you step forward in courage because you've decided that making an impact is more important than your fear of the outcome.

2. Making a difference requires stepping away from the sidelines, taking a risk, and trusting God in order to catalyze a response and movement in others.

3. When we love others, we overcome our own fears and objections and engage with them in meaningful ways.

CHAPTER 8

MORE THAN JUST YOU:
Transform Your Key Relationships

In this book, we've seen how a life of something more is possible. We learned that God originally intended for humanity to experience much more than we currently settle for. However, our journey is made difficult by our own sin and our broken and fallen world. In order to experience God's design we must grow closer to God and relate with Him personally and regularly. We

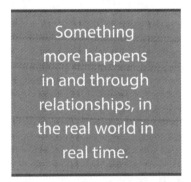

Something more happens in and through relationships, in the real world in real time.

must be intentional about our efforts and not try to do it alone. We must realize our potential and utilize our gifts to make a real difference in the lives of others. That last part—impacting the lives of others—is maybe the most misunderstood. This journey is not about reaching some point of mental and spiritual bliss. You will not float up to the sky or discover the life God intends in a cave on top of a mountain. Something more happens in and through relationships, in the real world in real time. It happens as we engage with our world, not separate from it. It is refined and expanded as we participate and partner with others in our quest.

You may have imagined you could pursue a "something more" faith separately from the rest of your life. Isn't that how many of us have approached faith in the past? Church is a place we go. We act holy at church or around church people, but we turn off our Christianity on Monday morning. Could that be the reason that the behavioral statistics for Christians are close to identical to those for non-Christians? Do we allow our faith to impact our everyday lives?

The reason we feel like we're missing something is that we are! Some of us have put on more faith than others, but it's still something we put on rather than who we are. Attending or engaging with faith is not the same as living it. The previous chapters in this book were intended to define, demonstrate, and develop the life God offers through a relationship with Himself. In this chapter, I want to get practical about our relationships with other people.

Something more is not just for you and God. Every relationship in our lives will benefit when we start living our faith. And you and I will get to enjoy fulfilling relationships, not only with God but with others. Let's consider just four key relationships: self, marriage, family, and work. I realize that not everyone has all four of these relationships, but this chapter is still for you. Consider how each section might apply to your own life and might help you benefit and encourage others.

In each section, we'll discuss two main ideas. First, we'll look at how our usual approach to each relationship falls short of God's vision. Second, we'll identify ways to pursue God's intention for each relationship. Taken together, these sections further define the life of a true follower of Jesus by the way she or he relates. I've found it fairly easy to be loving and not irritated when I'm by myself, but it's in relationships where we'll see whether this something more journey is really changing us. One of the first pastors I worked with used to say jokingly, "I'd love the ministry if it weren't for the people." Obviously the ministry is all about people. We can't control what others do, but if God is making a difference in our lives, our relationships with others should also be improved.

RELATIONSHIP TO SELF

We don't often think of "self" as a relationship, but it is. Our beliefs about and conversations with ourselves color our actions, behavior, and attitudes toward everyone and everything. Yet this important relationship is often built on a false idea of who we are.

When someone asks you who you are, what is the first thing that comes to mind? If you're like most people, it's likely either your occupation or season of life. You might say, "I'm a college student." "I'm a mom." "I'm a plumber, pastor, or small business owner." "I'm single, an empty nester, a grandparent." But these are not the labels God uses to identify you, and they're not how he wants you to define yourself. These labels can imprison us to a life of performance. We tend to rate ourselves on how well we're performing inside that definition either compared to others in similar circumstances or to our own image of success in that role. We beat ourselves up when we fall short and eventually burn ourselves out. The problem with all of these labels is that they are externals. They involve a set of expectations outside of ourselves and sometimes outside of our control. If our worth and identity are based on these externals, we will always be measuring ourselves against an image or ideal and feeling vulnerable to factors we can't control.

A few summers ago, I did a study of some of the key words and phrases God uses to describe us once we are His followers. As I examined each phrase in its context, I discovered that there were some places where I was living according to God's design. Yet there were several areas where I wasn't. My identity as seen through the eyes of God had become increasingly distant from the identity I was trying to create. When I surrendered some of my misperceptions and began living as if God's truth applied to me, I saw God's Spirit transform me in some exciting ways.

There are numerous phrases in the Bible that describe how God sees us as His creation. When we read the Scriptures where each phrase appears, and think about the implications, we'll begin to form a new understanding of our identity. I highly recommend taking some time over the next few months to focus on one word or phrase each week or so. Search the Bible, using a website like Bible Gateway (BibleGateway.com) or the YouVersion Bible app (YouVersion.com), and record your thoughts and discoveries in a notebook.

Allow me to share a few examples from my study. In 2 Corinthians 5:17, Paul tells us that anyone who is in Christ is a "new creation." This is freeing because it means we are not hindered by the past. But it also expresses the potential we discussed earlier. I get a fresh start, a new beginning, because of Jesus. Also, if I'm a new creation, that means I have a creator, which in turn means that I haven't earned who I am. I am *made* what I am. I'm made with certain wirings that God intends to be leveraged for good purposes—for growing in Christlikeness.

Another phrase that describes believers is "children of God," found in John 1:12, Romans 8:16, and Galatians 3:26, among other verses. This description has so many connotations. I'm a child, so I'm dependent. I'm innocent, wide-eyed, and open. I'm also bound to stumble as I learn. If I'm a child of God, I have godly DNA; I'm created in His image. If I'm God's child, He's my perfect Father. I can go to Him and He will fight for me, protect me, guide me, and always be there for me.

Still another example is the phrase "temple of God," found in 1 Corinthians 3:16: "Do you not know that you are a temple of God and that the spirit of God dwells in you?" (NASB). If I am a temple, a holy place, then I should live with purity and holiness. If am a place where God dwells and He is taking residence Inside of me, that means all of who He is can flow into me, through me, and out of me. He is the Prince of Peace, meaning I can be an agent of peace in my world. He is the Redeemer, meaning I can call upon His redeeming power in my relationships. For any aspect of God's character, when God dwells in us there is potential for us to exhibit His character in our daily lives.

What would happen if these were the labels we used to describe ourselves? What if this was our mindset? How might we treat others as new creations of Christ? How might we pray as children of God? How might we handle our dating relationships as temples of God? When we define ourselves as God defines us, it shapes the way we live.

So if our understanding of "self" falls short of God's vision, how do we pursue God's intention? A good starting point is to change how we communicate. We engage in a lot of damaging self-talk. Think about the things you tell yourself after a failure. Think about how you talk to yourself when something good happens. Think about the words you speak in your heart when you face a challenge. We may be aware of our thoughts, but I'm guessing that few of us challenge the conversation. We've become accustomed to living with ourselves and assume that if we tell ourselves something, it must be true.

I've recently become very aware of what I'm saying to myself. For several years, I've struggled with anxiety, particularly around my public ministry but in other areas too. As I began to explore this with some gifted and godly counselors, I discovered that many of the things I was saying to myself were lies. These things weren't true, but because they'd formed the soundtrack in my brain for so long, I assumed they were valid. Once I started examining my self-communication, I saw how it was impacting my anxiety and my attitude toward God and others.

For example, I remember one of the first times I became conscious of my anxiety. It was Christmas time and I had encouraged the congregation to invite their friends to a particular church service. Before that service, several people approached me to share stories. One told me that a coworker they had been inviting to church for five or six years had finally said yes and was in the room that day. Another told me of a widow who had not been to church in over forty years and who was there that day. The lie I heard was, "You'd better hit this sermon out of the park because the salvation of these people is on you!" Nothing could have been further from the truth, but I allowed myself to carry that weight and, though it wasn't evident to others, had a panic attack while I was preaching! I discovered how powerfully my thoughts could affect the rest of my body. My belief that life depended on my performance and success drove me away from the freedom God intended for me. Today, as I continue to replace lies with truth and despair with hope, I am excited to experience that freedom.

I pray the same for you. I believe you too will find some thoughts about yourself that need to be challenged and corrected. This could be the topic of a whole other book, but it starts with shifting the voice in your mind from the subconscious to the conscious, and from your own thoughts about you to God's thoughts about you. As you undertake this, receive God's grace and be kind and patient with yourself. Let the picture of God's design for your identity deliver you to freedom and true life.

MARRIAGE

We clearly can't cover the complexities of marriage in a few pages, but I hope this section will encourage you that something more is possible and give you the first steps in working toward it. Let's start where we did in the previous section and discuss how we think about marriage. What is its purpose? Understanding God's vision for marriage will give us clarity and help motivate us to pursue it.

In *The Meaning of Marriage,* Tim Keller defines marriage as: "a lifelong, monogamous relationship between a man and a woman. According to the Bible, God devised marriage to reflect his saving love for us in Christ, to refine our character, to create stable human community for the birth and nurture of children, and to accomplish all this by bringing the complementary sexes into an enduring whole-life union."

Maybe that definition is a little technical, but note one thing it doesn't mention: happiness. When the marriage relationship is working right, a peace and happiness pervades our lives. But when we make happiness the *goal* of our marriage, we miss out on its deeper intentions and the real joy that it could bring. We may make decisions that work against the more profound purposes God has in mind for our marriage. When simple happiness is our goal, we don't say the hard but loving things we need to say because the other person may not be happy with us. We may be tempted to suppress negative feelings or even walk away from the relationship because we're no longer happy.

Too many of us settle for happiness when God calls us to much more. God wants to use marriage to shape us and make us holy. He wants to create a partnership that accomplishes His purpose for His glory. It's in marriage that our sin is exposed more frequently than in any other relationship, so that we can confess and overcome it together. It's in marriage that we have the potential for the deepest level of community – for being known, loved, and served at points of real need and vulnerability. As both a pastor and a counselor, my heart aches for the sheer number of married people I see, even inside the church, who settle for such a small picture of marriage. God has a great vision for your marriage. Let's not settle for something small when something more is available to us.

So how do we put this understanding into practice? Again, communication is a good place to start. I've heard people list the top reasons for divorce as things like finances, sex, or relatives. But I believe communication is the root cause in many cases.

If you can communicate values, priorities, and expectations about finances, sex, or relatives, you can begin to work through problems. And if you can't communicate well, even simple things can cause conflict. This not only destroys happiness, but also God's greater purposes, and can often lead to divorce. That's why the one skill I recommend that every couple work on is communication. You may want to refer back to Chapter 5 on biblical community, as it contains a section on effective communication. Let me offer some additional suggestions that I've found helpful in counseling married couples.

1. Communicate with the other person in mind.
This seems obvious, but how many of us truly think about the person we're talking to? We speak in order to present our point of view, but communication is more than just airing one side. Communication involves a "sender" and a "receiver." If the sender has no regard for the receiver, the receiver will miss what the sender is saying. Yes, the receiver has a responsibility to listen – and most of us need work in this area too. But the sender who fails to consider the receiver's perspective will miss key opportunities for understanding.

2. Communicate in "I" language, not "you" language.
This may seem like a contradiction of my previous point, but it's not. Using "I" statements can be an act of humility, especially in times of conflict or when communicating about touchy subjects. It comes down to accusations and assumptions. We often assume we know *why* someone did or said something, and from that assumption we accuse the other of negative

motives. We say things like, "You always do such-and-such," in reference to some objectionable behavior. This approach is unlikely to result in immediate humility and confession by the hearer. Instead, the hearer, feeling under attack, will put up walls or lash back with an escalating rejoinder. But using a statement like "I feel _____ when you _____. Is that what you intend?" can disarm a potentially charged environment. And assuming your spouse loves you, then sharing your feelings—"I feel scared, lonely, or awkward when you say or do such-and-such"—will likely create compassion instead of defensiveness, producing a more meaningful dialogue.

3. Communicate to build the best possible version of the other person.

Ephesians 5 says we are to interact in ways that bring out holiness and blamelessness in our spouse. If that is our goal, we must intentionally say and do things that positively influence our partner. I want my wife, Lisa, to be able to say that she is a better person because she is married to me, and vice versa. We work toward that end in our relationship. When we are at our best, we encourage each other when we need to be encouraged, risk confronting each other when we need to be confronted, and set godly examples for each other as much as we can.

> God made our families for something more than acquiescing to the drama.

Again, I could say so much more on this topic. For further reading, I recommend Tim Keller's *The Meaning of Marriage* and Gary Thomas's *Sacred Marriage*. Within the context of this book, the point is that there is likely something more for you to experience in your marriage. When you and you and your spouse understand God's purpose in bringing you together, and then commit to pursuing that purpose, you'll be on your way to experiencing it. And communicating with grace and intentionality will serve you well along the way.

FAMILY

Everyone I've met can tell the story of some family drama. I've lived and witnessed my share and counseled those who are in the middle of it. But do you know what is really troubling about family drama? Everyone assumes that it will always be there. Instead of facing it and striving to resolve it, we avoid talking about it and work around it. We say things like, "That's just how she is" or "He won't listen, so let's not say anything." We settle for a family that is far from the way God designed it to be. And lest you think I don't live in the real world and can't possibly understand your family's unique dysfunction, let's remember that every family is full of sinners—and that includes me. I understand why, in dealing with people we can't control, we might resign ourselves to "that's just the way it is." But if we resign ourselves, we are ignoring what this book is all about: something more. God made our families for something more than acquiescing to the drama. They may never be all they could be, but I guarantee they can be better. As in the previous sections, growth will require some shifts in our thinking.

When it comes to our families, our biggest mindset errors are the things we settle for. First, we settle for *outwardly getting along.* Internally, we may be hurting, angry, or bitter, but we've come to believe that an outward appearance of peace is the highest ideal in family life. Second, we focus on *acceptable behavior,* particularly as parents. We use control and manipulation to manage our kids' behavior. As long as they are not visibly out of line, we call it good. Third, we focus on *performance and success.* None of us wants anyone in our family to fail, but sometimes we apply an inordinate amount of pressure to perform well, make money, and get ahead in the world. And finally, we adopt *cultural values.* We're all about self, happiness, and consumption as our highest ideals.

These four values are common among "normal" families, but they fall short of God's vision. His vision is not normal, but holy. We need to make some shifts in what we value as families. When we align our values with God's values, we'll see something more closely resembling God's design because our behaviors and conversations will be pursuing a different goal. Before we move on to practical steps, let's consider which of the four mindsets you've seen in your family. How have you seen those mindsets in action?

Now that we've shifted our thinking, let's look at some behavioral shifts that will move us toward something more in our families. Luke 12:13-21 tells the story of a man who approaches Jesus to settle a dispute about the inheritance he and his brother are due. Jesus proceeds to discuss wealth and our attitudes toward it, which is typically the theme when this passage is taught. But I think this story has something to offer in terms of family relationships. Notice how Jesus talks to this man. He refuses to render a verdict but invites him to reflect on the heart rather than the actions of his brother. The man who speaks to Jesus is focused on his brother's behavior and the money he's missing. Jesus reminds him that their dispute is a heart issue, not a money issue. His approach represents our first key shift: *from behavior to the heart.*

If we settle for outwardly getting along (behavior) while we're carrying around all kinds of junk (heart), our relationships will suffer. It's time to look deeper. As a parent when your kids act up, ask yourself, "What is this behavior accomplishing for them?" When a family member hurts or offends you, ask, "What beliefs about life does this behavior reflect?" When you shift to the heart, you can begin to heal underlying issues. We need to help others see their own hearts and what's driving them. As a parent, for example, discipline should always aim to teach, not control or create some form of outward compliance. We must learn to value heart change far more than outward compliance. And the better we understand our own hearts, the more clearly we'll see the real cause of conflict in our relationships. (See James 4:1-12.)

Our second behavioral shift is *from performance to acceptance and grace.* We've all felt the pressure to perform and get it right. But what if we created environments where people knew they were valued for who they are and not just what they do? Husbands, does your wife know you love her beyond the roles she plays? Wives, does your husband feel accepted and honored by you even if he doesn't complete the job the way you wanted him to?

Here's what happens when we focus on performance: We promote either entitlement or despair. The people in our lives feel entitled because they've performed up to our expectations or despair because our expectations were so high they could never reach them. Acceptance means believing the best about another person rather than assuming the worst—not regarding their performance but their value. It's seeking to understand before being understood. How many lectures have I given or received without real understanding of the person on the other side and the things that motivated his behavior? Just like God's grace, our grace should promote growth and forward movement in the lives of others. (See Titus 2:11-14.)

Our final shift applies especially to Christian families. We must move *from assumed to intentional faith.* I love how Deuteronomy 6:4-9 discusses God's plan for family faith. Verses 6-9 say this: "And these words that I command you today shall be on your heart. You shall teach them diligently to your children, and shall talk of them when you sit in your house, and when you walk by the way, and when you lie down, and when you rise. You shall bind them as a sign on your hand, and they shall be as frontlets between your eyes. You shall write them on the doorposts of your house and on your gates." Notice how the author emphasizes action: teach them diligently, talk of them, write them. Faith cannot be assumed; it must be intentionally cultivated. Our kids learn more from what we get excited about, what we talk about, and what we do than all our lectures combined.

This means sharing our faith stories with each other. What if even as adults we discussed with our siblings or adult children what God is teaching us? What if we prayed more together as families? As a church person, I'm amazed at how behaviors we are comfortable doing at church or in a small group are absent from our family interactions. We must learn to worship God together, depend on Him together, and invite Him into our lives together. Sometimes it's simply the way we talk about our relationship with God that begins to open the minds of others who have been accustomed to religious experiences without the relational component.

WORK

We spend a lot of our lives at our jobs, and if the concepts in this book are to be integrated into our lives, we must bring them into the workplace. Once again, let's start with our mindset. There

> Work is a calling by God to engage positively in our world.

are a number of ways people think about work. Some see it as drudgery, a necessary evil. These are the folks who need 47 cups of coffee to make it to lunch. Some see work as an opportunity to get ahead, to pay for vacations and expensive belongings, and to feel successful. Others see work as their identity, defining themselves by what they do. Finally, particularly in the church world, some see work as secular or unspiritual. You've read enough of this book to know that there's an issue with each of those mindsets.

The reality is that God created us to work, and the frustration we may feel is the result of sin (Genesis 3:17-19). But work itself is not sinful, nor is it a result of sin. And it certainly is not a punishment. God gave us meaningful work before sin entered into our world. Work is a calling by God to engage positively in our world. So we must give God the lead regarding why and how we work. That is the only way we will ever work by God's design. As Paul wrote in Colossians 3:23: "Whatever you do, work heartily, as for the Lord and not for men...." Now I looked up the word "whatever" in the original Greek, and do you know what that word actually means? Yup, you guessed it: Whatever! It doesn't matter so much what work you do but that whatever it is, you do it as for the Lord! We don't work to define our identity. We don't work to get ahead. We don't work as a necessary evil. We work as for the Lord!

> If faith does not impact every aspect of our lives, is it true faith?

So what does that attitude look like practically? First, *make the most of where you are.* You may not like where you are right now, but if you believe that God is sovereign, you must ask what He wants to do in and through you right where you are. When I was in college, I was so anxious to get out and start doing what I was being trained to do that I missed opportunities to build the most Kingdom value from my college experience.

There is a difference between our vocation and our occupation. Our vocation is what we are wired and called to do, while our occupation provides a living for ourselves and others. It's great when the same work meets both definitions. But the reality is that sometimes we must work an occupation while or until we fulfill our vocation. So make the most of where you are, but don't stop looking for opportunities to live out your vocation, either as a volunteer or professionally.

Second, *approach your work as sacred.* We don't want to compartmentalize our faith from our work (or from any other aspect of life, as we've seen throughout this book). God does not regard what we do in the secular world as any less valuable than what we do in ministry. If faith does not impact every aspect of our lives, is it true faith? When we approach our work as sacred, we recognize that God delights in good craftsmanship, in work done well. And as we work, in whatever work we do, we are to exercise the highest levels of integrity because we serve a holy God. We work hard because we're grateful for the ability to add value to an enterprise and to provide for our families. We may even have missional opportunities that God ordains in our workplace.

Finally, *invite God into what you do and how you do it.* I encourage you to begin your workday in prayer. Ask God what He wants to do with your day. Surrender your own aspirations to God's will and direction. Pray for energy to work hard and wisely. Pray for courage to walk blamelessly and speak up when needed. Ask God to help you serve the people you work with as if you were serving Him. Work in a way that represents Jesus, a way that makes others wonder why you work as wholeheartedly as you do. God cares deeply about what we do and how we do it. And He sees the challenges and frustrations we face. Some of these may be rectified by speaking the truth with grace. Some frustrations may fade as you find your sweet spot in your current job or another occupation. In any case, inviting God into your work will give you His wisdom as you face any challenge.

As we wrap up this chapter, remember that my intention was not an exhaustive discussion of each of our key relationships. I highly recommend seeking out additional books and resources that may assist you in these relationships. Personally, I have also found a godly counselor to be helpful in showing me things I couldn't see myself and pointing me to a better way. My heart is to see a something more mindset permeate everything we do. We often settle for less in our relationships, but God wants to transform not just our spiritual experience but all of our lives. As you look at the relationships that mean the most to you, can you identify some areas you've resigned yourself to accept as just the way they are? Can you imagine what they would look like if they were operating closer to God's design? Let's make God's vision our own and start seeking something more in our relationships.

SUMMING IT UP

1. Something more is not just between you and God. Every relationship in our lives will benefit when we start living our faith.

2. Transforming our relationships means acknowledging that our usual approach falls short of God's vision and purpose.

3. God's Word provides guidance as we pursue His intention for our relationship with ourselves, our marriages, our families, and our work.

CHAPTER 9

MORE INFLUENCE:
Envision a "Something More" Church

In my high school psychology class, we did something called "the shaping exercise" to demonstrate how people can be influenced by the affirmation and leading of others. The teacher sent a student into the hallway and had the class decide on an action we wanted that student to perform. We decided we wanted our classmate to stand in the garbage can. The catch was that we couldn't use any words, only applause or silence. The student re-entered and stood at the front of the room. Then he moved slightly in the direction of the garbage can, and we all applauded. When he moved away again, we gave him our silence. Step by step, he approached the garbage can. Then he put his hand in the garbage can, and we applauded loudly. Finally, without any words, we were able to convince him to step into the garbage can. I wouldn't have believed it if I hadn't seen it myself.

A good leader can inspire others to move in the desired direction even without words.

In addition to the intended lesson about people's willingness to follow, this illustration impressed on me the power of a leadership that affirms others. A good leader can inspire others to move in the desired direction even without words. Among other things, Jesus was a leader and His leadership often reflected this approach. He believed in people and called them to what they could become. In a sense Jesus' leadership was inviting people to experience something more.

Can you imagine leading a whole church to live out the principles we've discussed in this book? Can you imagine a large group of people pursuing the kinds of relationships we've envisioned? What if our small groups and communities were populated by genuine, active, all-in, Jesus-following people? If that vision excites you, how might you help make it so?

I have two audiences in mind for this chapter. First, I'm talking specifically to church leaders about developing a something more mindset within a church. But if you're not a church leader, don't skip this chapter! My suggestions are for you too. These leadership lessons apply to families, workplaces, small groups, ministry teams, and all groups working together for a common purpose. And maybe you can introduce these ideas to your church pastor, too!

Much has been written about leadership, but in a world that's crying out for godly leaders we can't overemphasize these principles. It's rare to meet someone who's never served as a leader in any way. Even if you're that rare individual, read this chapter and pray for your leaders! God uses effective leaders to help us grow. The following guidelines can help build effective leaders and motivate and inspire movement among the whole church.

1. Have transformation as your clear destination.
Since my family lives in Minnesota and all our relatives are on the East Coast, we've taken several road trips over the past

decade. Each time, we've taken a different route so we could see other parts of the country, stop at various landmarks, and experience new scenery. But regardless of our route, we

> The Bible was given not just to inform us but to transform us.

always have a clear destination. We type the destination into our GPS, and we know we'll end up where we want to go.

If you don't know where you're going, it's hard to know when you have arrived, and it's even harder to motivate people to leave the place they are now and follow you. While some leaders convince people to follow them based on charisma alone, most folks want to know where you're headed before they're willing to follow. If you're not clear on your destination, few will follow. And as they say, a leader without followers is not really a leader—he's just a guy going for a walk.

On the journey toward something more, the destination is all about transformation. The Bible was given not just to inform us but to transform us. One reason people have become disenchanted by church is that they were not offered a compelling destination or even the transformation that happens along the way. The sad thing is that many churches have great teachers, the best programs, and excellent discipleship materials, but they've squandered it all by emphasizing information over transformation. And so we have uncounted thousands of Christians with a lot of head knowledge who don't know how to love their families or act with integrity in their jobs or handle conflict with grace and authenticity.

While transformation is a broad topic, it does provide clarity of focus, a destination, a goal by which to evaluate everything we do. The Apostle Paul often said things like, "We are responsible to present you to God as pure, holy, essentially transformed." (See Colossians 1:24-29.) When evaluating programs, events, and sermon topics, it's essential to ask: Does this move us toward transformation? How? Will we better love Jesus and love others as a result?

2. Expose the tensions.

Our churches won't be transformed if the people we lead don't take responsibility for their own growth. One of the challenges of leadership is creating "buy-in." We've all met leaders who try to accomplish this through guilt, but guilt rarely motivates someone to change. And even when change occurs, guilt doesn't produce the long-term growth we long to see.

I've found that a better way to motivate is to expose tensions. The kind of tension I'm talking about is created in one of two ways: Either two opposite things pull at us from different directions or there's a gap between where we are and where we want to be. Often people experience tension but aren't sure *why* they're feeling it. A leader can expose the source of tension by asking questions. Questions prompt listeners to consider their personal experience and raise curiosity about what the speaker will say next.

For example, a leader might ask, "Have you ever felt like no matter what you do you can't seem to make anyone happy, and you doubt whether God is happy with you either?" This question exposes the tension caused by competing expectations and suggests a spiritual component that may not have been obvious. Look for any question that brings tension to the forefront: "Does it ever seem like everybody else is tracking, but you feel like you're missing something?" "Have you ever been bored with your faith or wondered if there is anything of value in it?" Most of us don't enjoy tension and, when it is exposed, will look for resolution. We ask ourselves, "How do I get rid of this?" Or worse, "How can I ignore it or cover it up?" Instead we want to move people to seek the wisdom and courage—from the Scriptures, the Spirit, and their leaders—to work through the tension and reach the place they need to be.

Exposing tension moves individuals to take action, and it can influence the church as a whole too. Maybe certain ministries or events are failing to take people where they need to go. Maybe church members feel collectively stuck or frustrated or bored. As church leaders, we can expose this tension and create a sense of urgency and desire to move forward. One reason churches stagnate is that they

Programs aren't bad in themselves, but we must ensure that they are part of a process.

won't admit they're stuck. A courageous leader will expose the tension, humbly admit the need, and call fellow leaders to action —maybe reading a book together, bringing in a consultant, or attending a conference. Whether at the individual or group level, trying to bring change without exposing the tension is like trying to drag or push an elephant. I've not tried it, but I think you'd either get stepped on or pooped on.

3. Let programs derive from process.

Andy Stanley, in his ministry classic *7 Practices of Effective Ministry*, coined the phrase *think steps, not programs*. In churches, programs can take on a life of their own. Often a program that was intended to serve a greater purpose becomes something we're managing for its own sake. If we think about the steps required for growth and create the best environments for those steps, we will facilitate movement, not just fill programs. Programs aren't bad in themselves, but we must ensure that they are part of a process, with every program leading to the next one. Otherwise our programs become stopping points rather than places of movement.

Several years ago, our church undertook the process of evaluating our long list of ministry programs. None of these programs were bad in themselves, but there were a few things we noticed. One was that several programs were essentially trying to do the same things, so we were diluting our resources and maintaining more than was necessary.

Second, there were some programs that had either forgotten their purpose or begun operating without real accountability to the larger vision of the church. We addressed this by clarifying our purpose and reinventing some programs. While this upset the apple cart (and some of our people), it was necessary to get us all moving in the same direction.

The third thing we noticed is that we were missing steps, meaning that it would be difficult for someone to move from one program to the next. For example, our small group program required people to move directly from attending worship services to joining a close-knit group that had met, or would meet, for years. To create an intermediate step, we launched a four-week group for newcomers and trial groups for regular attenders who weren't part of an existing small group.

The point is to evaluate whether the current programs, and the process that connects them, moves people forward, and then to revise, remove, or reinvent as needed.

4. Commit to simplicity.

We touched on this in the previous paragraphs, but let me add this: As churches, we must limit what we offer because people will view every activity as equal. Even the people inside each ministry will expect equal time, attention, and support—financial, pastoral, and volunteer.

But the reality is that not all activities are equal. Some are critical steps that people must take in their spiritual growth. Others are less essential. Some are outdated and out of touch. And some are even at odds with the mission and vision of the church, continuing on through inertia or unwillingness to ruffle the feathers of legacy adherents.

When we offer too many choices, people are likely to become overwhelmed and choose nothing or to overlook opportunities that would most benefit their growth. This is an ongoing challenge for church leadership. There are lots of great ideas out there, and we'd love to try them all. But our commitment to clarity and simplicity compels us to say no to the good for the sake of the best—meaning what's best for growth.

5. Develop a common language.

An effective but often overlooked strategy for fostering a shared vision is to develop a shared language. Our church has worked intentionally to develop meaningful terms and phrases that communicate our "brand" or way of thinking. Other phrases emerge from sermons and end up sticking with us. For example, several years ago I said during a sermon, "As a church we want to create disciples not donors. We're not interested in people who give donations to God's church but seek people who prioritize generosity because of their relationship with God." Some of our elders adopted that language, and it began to show up in conversations: "We're not looking for donations around here; we want you to grow as a disciple. If enough of our people do that, the church's financial needs will be met." A single sermon provided the language to reframe our thinking around finances and giving.

We've probably used more than 30 such phrases in different seasons in our church, to help clarify what we're about and unify us in a common direction. Many of the phrases are similar, so people aren't moved in 30 directions, but language gives them different "hooks" to hang their understanding on. As you develop language around the concepts in this book, choose phrases that are memorable and portable, short enough that people can take them into their conversations. As we all start using them, the language becomes scaffolding for the culture we want to create.

6. Build connections.

In a "something more" church, faith can't be an individual pursuit. You can preach sermons, write devotionals, and recommend books, but unless you connect people to each other, you'll only inspire individual spiritual growth. Ultimately, such growth is stunted because we need each other to reach our full potential. Connecting people through study and fellowship groups, or smaller clusters of two to three "traveling partners," will expand

and strengthen your church's movement toward transformation. Like the wheel ruts from a wagon train, our movement forward will leave a deeper mark if we're moving together.

When we engage together around our shared faith, we encounter experiences and perspectives unlike our own. Small groups also add a level of authenticity and accountability. The simple fact that we are getting together to talk about something more will encourage us to keep pursuing it.

7. Make evaluation the norm.

Even the best programs and ideas can lose their way. Some even lose their relevance to the church's current situation. In our church, we constantly ask ourselves, "Why are we doing this? How does it move us along the path of transformation?" If the answer is inadequate, the program goes back to the workshop for evaluation, clarification, and In some cases removal.

The hard thing is that the staff and key leaders who direct these ministries may take such questions and comments personally. They may feel their particular ox is being unfairly gored. One way to mitigate this is to consistently and regularly evaluate all ministry programs. That way, evaluation becomes a norm and nothing is allowed to go too far without course correction. We must regularly communicate that everything has a season, that change is necessary for effective ministry, and that programs can have both a sunrise and a sunset. People need time to process change. As much as possible, we should include key people in the development of new programs and allow ample time before implementing major changes, including the sunsetting of programs that have run their course.

8. Eliminate sideways energy.

Sideways energy is energy devoted to things that, while they may be good in themselves, don't forward an organization's mission or vision. I've seen this happen in churches often, and it's so difficult to address. I've worked with staff who were gifted in certain areas and passionate about certain activities that fell (or have fallen) outside the focus of the church's forward movement. They had the skills to develop programs and initiatives that could have a big impact in another context. But they did not advance the current vision of the church.

The reason this is so difficult is that many of these sideways endeavors have real value. We're not saying no to them because they're inherently wrong; they simply fall outside the areas we're prioritizing. Or perhaps one person is very excited about a particular program, but the rest of the leadership team doesn't share that excitement. That one person may plunge in and get things done while the rest of the team is committed and fruitful elsewhere. Again, it is probably not a bad ministry, but it's not one that God is calling the group to pursue at this time. These are slippery decisions, but they are important ones. If we don't eliminate sideways energy we end up diluting our vision and the energy needed to achieve it. We'll have churches that offer a little bit of everything without focusing on anything.

9. Stay the course.

One of the most challenging aspects of church leadership is simply staying the course. As church leaders, we will be inundated with great ideas, many of which we'll adopt. But we need to guard against embracing too many ideas, especially ones that change our trajectory. You may have known a pastor who revamped the church with every new book he read or conference he attended. Trust is built when we stay true to our vision, incorporating new ideas and new language beneath a stable umbrella.

And we must stay the course even when we're not seeing progress. There will be people who try to sway or discourage us, but we must persevere. We found in our church that when we were stagnant and not growing, it wasn't time to abandon our vision but to bring it into sharper focus. By clarifying what was previously vague and strategizing to make vision reality, we entered a season of growth that we hadn't experienced before.

10. Adjust alignment.

As a pastor for more than 20 years and a lead pastor for more than ten, I've observed that if church leadership is not aligned, forward movement is incredibly difficult. That should come as no surprise, but how do we bring alignment? Here are a few ideas that have worked in my experience.

First, bring in common content that doesn't originate from you. Together with your other leaders, read a book, watch a video series, or attend a conference together. This introduces an impartial voice of wisdom. Then provide time and space to discuss and digest what you've read or observed. For example, you might all read a book like *Something More*,

> Imagine the impact if an entire church got serious about embracing something more.

discussing a chapter each week and how it might be applied within the context of your church. Because it's an outside voice, no one worries that criticism will be taken personally, and even the facilitator can disagree with the content. You are all seeking the best path forward for the team and the church you serve together, not necessarily adopting the content in its entirety.

I also suggest candidly discussing alignment and what alignment looks like. Too often alignment and unity are assumed, instead of intentionally pursued. Our church's alignment discussions have led us to develop common language, clarify priorities, and work on strategy together.

—⁓—

The pursuit of something more benefits individuals. It also benefits teams and churches when individuals gather together to work through these concepts. Imagine the impact if an entire church got serious about not settling for a stagnant faith but embracing something more. For that to happen, we need godly and capable leaders to lead us along a journey of transformation —of something more.

The people in our churches, as well as those who don't know Jesus, are longing for something authentic and life changing. If we focus on helping people become Christians but don't provide tools for serious growth, we diminish what being a Christian means and inadvertently make our faith less attractive than it really is. When we lead people to something more, we extend Jesus' invitation to a transformational, life-altering faith.

SUMMING IT UP

1. A something more movement requires effective leadership.

2. To inspire movement, effective leaders must have a clear destination, expose tensions, derive programs from process, commit to simplicity, develop a common language, and build connections.

3. To mobilize a leadership team, effective leaders make evaluation the norm, eliminate sideways energy, stay the course, and adjust the team's alignment.

CHAPTER 10

MORE TO COME:
Make God's Dream Your Dream

Postcards were popular when I was young. I remember collecting postcards with pictures of the places we visited on vacation. There were pictures of the Statue of Liberty, a beautiful sunset at the beach, and my favorite Disney characters. While I simply collected postcards, others actually mailed these cardstock pictures to people who were not on vacation. Many postcards featured clever sayings related to the location, but the most common phrase was "wish you were here." I never understood that. It was like, "Hey, we're having a great time at this amazing location without you. We thought we'd send you a picture of this place that you're not at so you could feel even worse that you're stuck at boring old home! Isn't it awesome that we're on vacation and didn't invite you?" Okay, that's a little sarcastic, but I wasn't sure how the person receiving the card could have thought differently.

Believing the best of the postcard designers, maybe the intention was, "We think you'd love this place and now that we're here, we wish you could have somehow been here with us!" And so, with the best possible intentions, I say to you, "I wish you were here." I'm not talking about a vacation that temporarily removes you from reality, but a new relationship and connection with God, yourself, fellow believers, and the world at large. I wish for you a life of something more that God intends for us all. And I don't want it to be an escape or a temporary move. I want it to be for you, as it has been for me, a transforming lifestyle.

Sometimes when we hear the word "more," we think of something beyond the original plan, or beyond what most people get to experience. But the "more" we've been talking about is God's intended norm. We are the ones who've drifted from it, settling for something less, or covering it up in legalism, ritual, and routine. Something more is part of God's mission and design. It's not only how He intends to connect with His creation, but it's how He intends for His redeemed children to make their mark in the world.

GOD'S DREAM FOR HIS PEOPLE

I love how The Message version of the Bible translates 1 Peter 2:21: "This is the kind of life you've been invited into, the kind of life Christ lived. He suffered everything that came his way so you would know that it could be done, and also know how to do it, step-by-step." When we look at the context of the entire chapter, we see a call from Peter to live as we were designed regardless of the pushback from our culture. We are chosen by God. As God's people, you and I are intended to show something different to the world.

But we should also know that this journey is not without its challenges, both suffering and persecution or pushback from the world. The book of 1 Peter shows the harsh realities of choosing to live for God, and I can't leave this book without acknowledging those realities. I would never trade this life of something more for anything, but it is not without difficulties.

There are the universal challenges of living in a fallen world, like sickness, natural disaster, and sinful people. There are challenges to live in holiness as we are bombarded with everything except what is pleasing to God.

And then there are the challenges of engaging a world that will continue to grow further from God's design and will be increasingly intolerant of our commitment to live for Him. I can't imagine enduring these things without the presence, love, and power of God in me and with me. When we try to do the Christian life on our own, and in our own strength, we miss the very things that God has given us to face the challenges. I plead with you not to walk alone, not to settle, and not to give up when it's hard. Though there's pain on the journey, the destination is worth it.

Whether it's some form of suffering, trial, or disappointment, or whether it's persecution of any form because of your faith, this pursuit is difficult. In some ways it might seem easier to blend in and avoid it altogether. But remember that the life we are pursuing is worth it and that the difficulty we face might be leveraged for God's purposes. God may want to redeem it to continue transforming a piece of our character. He may want to use the experience to provide blessing, comfort, or empathy toward others.

When I face difficulty, I make an effort to ask myself three questions. First, is this difficulty the result of a bad decision or sin in my life? If so, I need to confess and repent. Second, is this an opportunity for God to shape or change a part of me that I've been ignoring or hiding from Him? And third, should I accept this as simply another reminder of the broken, fallen world in which I live? The question I've learned to stop asking is: Does this difficultly mean that God doesn't love me, has given up on me, or has failed me in some way? That question is straight from the evil one and has no place in the life of a Christian. You are loved—loved enough to die for—and the idea that God would fail us because He doesn't love us is foreign to everything in the Scriptures.

I want to explore one more Scripture with you before we finish. Ephesians 3:14-21 may be familiar to you, but it's worth rereading these verses in full:

> For this reason I bow my knees before the Father, from whom every family in heaven and on earth is named, that according to the riches of his glory he may grant you to be strengthened with power through his Spirit in your inner being, so that Christ may dwell in your hearts through faith—that you, being rooted and grounded in love, may have strength to comprehend with all the saints what is the breadth and length and height and depth, and to know the love of Christ that surpasses knowledge, that you may be filled with all the fullness of God.
>
> Now to him who is able to do far more abundantly than all that we ask or think, according to the power at work within us, to him be glory in the church and in Christ Jesus throughout all generations, forever and ever. Amen.

The Apostle Paul wrote this prayer to the Ephesians, whom he loved, because he wanted them to know his dream for them. The great news is, because Paul's dream was within God's will, he could depend on God to bring it about. Paul had made God's dream his dream. He wanted the Ephesians to be strengthened from the inside through the Spirit's work within them. He wanted them to know the presence of Jesus at all times. He wanted them to operate from a position of being loved and filled with all the fullness of God. The fullness of God is something far beyond my ability to comprehend or contain. How could I be even partially filled with the fullness of God? It's amazing!

At the end of this section, Paul reminds us that the God we serve is able to do much more than we could ever ask or imagine. Sit with that for a second. This picture of our God is not small. It is not legalistic. It is not based on performance or ritual or conformance. This is the picture of a vibrant, active, engaged, and loving God. This tells me that our something more is easy for God. It says that the life in Christ that I'm living now, however it may have grown, is not close to the life God has prepared for me and yearns for me to live. I hope that this picture captures

"Good enough" isn't good enough anymore.

your heart and imagination and inspires you to write the next chapter of this book! God is able to do *far more abundantly*. That sounds a lot like something more.

But let's not lose the context and purpose of that work. Paul says God's work is for His glory in the church and throughout generations. He will do the work in real time, in us, through us, and among us. It happens relationally and within community. It's not a bunch of unconnected individuals gaining more from God, but a church—a community—giving Him glory and experiencing His movement among them and through them. The purpose of His work is to glorify God. It's not about us achieving some level of prominence or significance. It's not a self-fulfillment scheme. It's about pointing it all back to God who deserves the glory for everything. It's about showing the world there is something worth glorifying and living for and that discovering Jesus and living by His power moves us to a whole new place.

Within that context, I want you to think with me: What is God's dream for you? What does God want for you? Can you bring yourself to imagine that God has a personal interest in your life involving a compelling purpose and a plan? How has He prepared you? Wired you? What experiences and people have shaped who you are today? How might He want to leverage who you've become to impact the world for His glory? Who would He have you rub shoulders with? Who would He have you connect with? What are the next steps He wants you to take?

The point is that something more is so much bigger than you and me. God is inviting us into a mission of never-ending possibilities. Yes, He wants us to grow and relate personally with Him, but not so that we can walk around bragging about our "walk with God." You and I need that kind of connection just to survive in a world so foreign to the things of God.

And that same world needs us to actively impact it as part of the global mission of God. We can't afford to settle in our faith. There is so much more at stake than just our personal feelings of fulfillment. You are so loved, so chosen, so prepared for what is ahead of you. Make God's dream your dream, and get ready for something more than you've ever imagined.

Listen, I don't want to "wish you were here." I've spent too long as a pastor wishing people would engage in this journey.

I've been tempted to lower the standards and settle for the way things are. But there's too much at stake. It's time for both you and me to move toward God's design for us. "Good enough" *isn't* good enough anymore. God is waking us up and calling us forward. I'm jumping into the wave, and I pray that you'll join me in His movement forward. For me and you. For His people. For the world. There is no more time for compromised lives, complacent faith, or foolish sin. Something more is waiting, and Someone more is inviting us to put down the postcard and experience the journey of a lifetime.

Growing up in a Christian family in New Jersey, Jason attended Hawthorne Gospel Church. There, he was fortunate to have several people invest in his growth. He had opportunity to serve in leadership roles beginning at age 10 in Christian Service Brigade, youth ministry, and Bible teaching at Top 'O the Hill Day Camp. He graduated from Philadelphia College of Bible (currently Cairn University) with a Bachelor's degree in Bible and served as a youth director for all four years of college. His first thirteen years of full-time ministry were all among students (middle school, high school, and college). During those years, he earned a Master's degree in Christian counseling/discipleship, worked as an adjunct faculty member at Nyack College, and started Nxt Ministries as an opportunity to train volunteer youth leaders and speak at retreats and rallies. He married his best friend, Lisa, in 1999 and together they've been serving God in various ministry roles. As a teaching pastor and now as a lead pastor, Jason has developed leaders, cast vision, crafted strategies, coached staff and leaders, and counseled couples and individuals.

His personal mission statement is all about maximizing the spiritual potential of individuals and organizations. He looks forward to opportunities to connect, teach, and coach. Jason is incredibly grateful to Jesus for His grace, mercy, and opportunity to serve others in His name!

www.lifeinprocess.com is Jason's website resource
with free articles on faith, family and leadership.

www.jasonstonehouse.com is Jason's church blog
where he writes on various subjects.

Connect with Jason on social media:
Twitter: @StonehouseJason
Instagram: @pastorjts